PETSCAPING

Training and Landscaping with Your Pet in Mind

SCOTT COHEN & CAROLYN DOHERTY

Schiffer Publishing Ltd

4880 Lower Valley Road   Atglen, Pennsylvania 19310

Other Schiffer Books on Related Subjects:

Designed by Justin Watkinson   Cover by Bruce Waters
Type set in Chalet-LondonNineteenSeventy/Zurich BT

ISBN: 978-0-7643-3854-0   Printed in China

Schiffer Books are available at special discounts
for bulk purchases for sales promotions or
premiums. Special editions, including
personalized covers, corporate imprints,
and excerpts can be created in large
quantities for special needs.
For more information contact the publisher:

Published by Schiffer Publishing Ltd.
4880 Lower Valley Road
Atglen, PA 19310
Phone: (610) 593-1777
Fax: (610) 593-2002
E-mail: Info@schifferbooks.com

For the largest selection of fine
reference books on this and related
subjects, please visit our website at
www.schifferbooks.com
We are always looking for people
to write books on new and related
subjects. If you have an idea for a
book, please contact us at
the above address.

This book may be purchased
from the publisher.
Include $5.00 for shipping.
Please try your bookstore first.
You may write for a free catalog.

In Europe, Schiffer books
are distributed by
Bushwood Books
6 Marksbury Ave.
Kew Gardens
Surrey TW9 4JF England
Phone: 44 (0) 20 8392 8585; Fax: 44 (0) 20 8392 9876
E-mail: info@bushwoodbooks.co.uk; Website: www.bushwoodbooks.co.uk

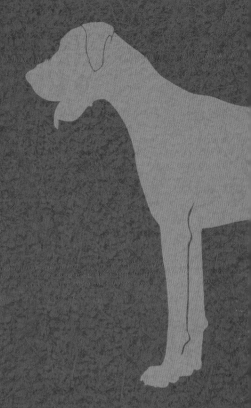

Contents

Welcome to **PETSCAPING**: *Training and Landscaping with Your Pet in Mind*. This book provides information, tips, and expertise for creating a fun, beautiful, safe, and stimulating backyard environment for your pets and family. The book is borne from 22 years of working with homeowners on residential landscape designs nationwide. As pets seem to have taken on a greater role in family life, my backyard designs have "gone to the dogs" to adapt.

Wherever I go, folks are always asking me for advice on how to design their yards to solve the challenges that sharing a yard with pets can present. The problem is, it is never just a landscape solution alone. Pets are people too, and our furry friends have their own personalities and behavioral issues to consider. The best solutions are always a combination of knowledgeable pet training and well planned landscape design. So how could I respond to their questions?

This book is the answer. I've joined up with long time friend and expert animal trainer Carolyn Doherty to create *Petscaping*. An idea that started out over a family dinner has grown to become a unique and rich resource on pet training and landscape design, tackling design and pet behavioral issues in the garden.

This book was written for pet lovers and the professionals that design for them. Enjoy!

Scott Cohen
Garden Artisan, The Green Scene & HGTV
scottcohendesigns.com
greenscenelandscape.com

As a professional animal trainer, I have helped owners work with their pets for nearly two decades. My approach to training is always twofold: provide the best possible situation for a pet, one that naturally encourages good behavior, and pair it with compassionate training to teach the pet what good behavior is. Although identifying what's not working and adapting a training program for each client comes naturally to me, advising clients on how to make the necessary changes to their yards is beyond my area of expertise. Time and again I've suggested consulting landscaping books for guidance, while I lamented that I did not know of the perfect one to recommend. Now with *Petscaping* in print, that's all changed, and I am honored to have worked with a pro like Scott on this fun and unique project!

There are many landscaping books and animal training books on the market, but *Petscaping* is the first to combine comprehensive information about creating the perfect outdoor environment for your pet with answers for behavioral questions that arise when a pet is outside. Each topic is addressed from both points of view and the answers are written with logic and simplicity in mind. We've broken down landscaping, gardening, and training into easy-to-understand explanations, with lots of charts, pictures, and time-saving tips, so you can quickly access the information you need. It has numerous project descriptions for the do-it-yourselfers as well as key design guidelines to aid landscaping professionals. And, as for the training, whether you're an experienced dog owner or you've just acquired your very first pooch, you'll be able to master the techniques with ease, and have a happy coexistence with your furry best friend in no time.

I'm excited to present this book to you, and hope you enjoy your hand at Petscaping!

Carolyn Doherty
Owner, Gracious Dog Obedience
www.GraciousDog.com

Design Considerations

What kind of woof?
Dog-specific considerations

Before you start designing, evaluate what your dog is like and what qualities may be important when planning your yard. For instance, the type of fence you require will differ greatly if you have an enthusiastic digger versus a playful companion dog. Consult the chart on page 10 for qualities to consider and examples of common breeds that tend to have those qualities. Remember, any dog can have any attribute, so pay attention not only to your dog's breed (or breeds, in the case of a mix) but what you've observed from him yourself.

These yards have been beautifully designed to provide optimum comfort for the pets and their owners.

◄ *Scott has his hands full because his young Beagle fits three of the following categories: High energy, highly intelligent and active, and potential digger or escape artist!*

Petscaping Your Yard

What kind of woof?

Type of Dog	Characteristic	Petscaping Considerations
Herding breeds Retrievers Terriers	High Energy	Maximize exercise space, include heavy duty pathways and groundcover (CHAPTER1)
Herding and Guard breeds Terriers Poodles	Highly intelligent and active	"Working" breeds thrive with tasks like agility courses and other active games (CHAPTER 5)
Bulldogs Hound Dogs Terriers	Digger or escape artist	Proper fencing and digging area are must-haves (CHAPTERS 1, 6)
Guard breeds such as Rottweilers, German Shepherds, Mastiffs, Akitas, Terriers	Territorial or aggressive	Protective fencing and obstructive shrubs prevent unwanted attacks (CHAPTERS 1, 6)
Poodles and water dogs Setters and Spaniels Retrievers and collies	Loves water and swimming	Consider a pool, pond, or fountain (CHAPTER4)
Cold weather breeds such as Malamutes, Huskies, Great Pyrenees, St. Bernards, Newfoundlands, Akitas	Heat Sensitive	Breeds with thick fur coats developed for frigid climates must have abundant shade and water sources (CHAPTER 4)

CHECK THE
DIRECTION OF
PREVAILING ⚠ E
WINDS

NORTH

SHADE
AREA ⚠ D

FEED &
WASHING
STATION
⚠ A

GARAGE
(FOOD STOR.)

SHARED FENCE;
COULD PRESENT
PROBLEM ⚠ F

NEIGHBOR'G LOT

CONTAINMENT SHOULD
HAVE FRONT LOT
EXPOSURE IF POSSIBLE ⚠ B

CHOOSE LOCATION
WITH OPTIMAL
DRAINAGE ⚠ C

PLAN TD ST.

Rough initial layout of yard areas:
The "Bubble Plan"

The first step in creating your Petscaped backyard is to create a rough initial layout, referred to as a "Bubble Plan." To create a "Bubble Plan" start with a clean piece of paper that has your home and property lines defined. The purpose of this exercise is to help visualize the influential design parameters (wind, sun, shade, traffic flow, views, etc.). Draw free-flowing shapes, circles or bubbles, to define the planned use of these areas. More specific measurements can be defined later in the design process.

When *"Petscaping"* your garden use this handy checklist to ensure you have taken all the basics into consideration and mapped them on your plan. While every home, garden and pet will have different specific conditions to accommodate, this checklist will help get you started.

PETSCAPING ZONES:

Choose an area in the yard for each of these items and mark them on your plan.

- ☑ Exercise and play
- ☑ Sleep
- ☑ Feeding stations
- ☑ Water stations
- ☑ Grooming station (utilities required?)
- ☑ Elimination
- ☑ Confinement – Is a dog run required?
- ☑ Shelter from the elements and predators
- ☑ Shade and Sun areas
- ☑ Edible garden

CONTAINMENT FENCING

How will the yard be fenced off to contain your pet?

OFF LIMIT AREAS

Define to which areas your pets are not allowed access.

Do multiple pets need to be kept away from each other?

BEWARE OF THE DOG

Choosing the Right Fence

CHAIN LINK | WROUGHT IRON
BLOCK WALLS | WOODEN FENCING
ELECTRIC FENCES | HEDGES

Chain link fencing comes with a long list of potential problems for your dog. First of all, the end of the fence (on top, bottom, and sides) where the links are cut often have sharp points; your dog can cut his face, body, and paws on this or get his collar hooked on one of these ends. Second, the holes between the links and the high visibility to the other side of the fence encourage dogs to chew on the mesh or put their snouts through the holes. This can lead to abrasions to the face and inside the mouth, and, with continued gnawing, can wear down their teeth. Being able to fit their entire snout through the holes can also encourage fence aggression towards people and other animals on the other side as they try to gain access. Lastly, many agile dogs hook their paws on the wires and climb up the mesh of a chain link fence, significantly hindering its purpose of keeping your dog in your yard!

▲ *Wrought iron fencing retains pets in the yard without obstructing impressive views.*

CHAIN LINK | WROUGHT IRON
BLOCK WALLS | WOODEN FENCING
ELECTRIC FENCES | HEDGES

Wrought iron fencing is a good choice for many reasons – it is durable, attractive, and immune to chewing. There are, however, some things to consider with respect to your particular dog. The wrought iron is usually constructed with a 4 inch gap between the bars. This is plenty of room for most small breeds to fit through, and definitely big enough for any dog's face to fit between the bars. Obviously, if your dog can fit through the bars, the fence is not going to serve its intended purpose. Likewise, if your dog can fit even his head through the bars, you open yourself up to a variety of problems resulting from access to whomever or whatever is on the other side of the fence. He can easily fence fight with neighboring dogs or injure people who get too close to the fence (think little kid's hands). Even if your dog is not aggressive, curiosity can put him on the receiving end of these same problems as he investigates what's out there.

The problem can be remedied when installing the fence by simply spacing the bars closer together. But what if the fence is pre-existing or your community dictates a uniform configuration? Then the problem can be addressed by adding additional pickets in the fence, screening the fence with welded wire mesh, or adding sheet metal or pinhole mesh.

▶ *The difference tighter spacing can make is obvious here, as this dog's head fits through the upper bars but not through the lower bars with the addition of more pickets at the bottom.*

▲ *Block walls offer permanent protection for your pets and are easy to screen with vines and shrubs.*

◄ *The security of this block wall is enhanced by adding a thick line of hedges between the yard and the fence.*

CHAIN LINK I WROUGHT IRON
BLOCK WALLS I WOODEN FENCING
ELECTRIC FENCES I HEDGES

It's hard to find fault with a block wall. They are strong and durable, do not fall prey to chewers, and are very difficult for a dog to climb. Block walls also discourage digging and other doggy destruction. In addition to providing some sound attenuation, the solid structure of a block wall offers excellent protection from the outside world.

Petscaping Your Yard

Wooden fences are a little bit of a gamble when used to enclose a canine. For most dogs, they work perfectly well; they are inexpensive, attractive, easy to erect, and the slats are traditionally spaced close enough together that paws and snouts don't fit through. There are a few potential problems, however, which should be carefully considered before choosing this type of fence. First of all, does your dog like to chew? Wooden slats quickly become the chew toy of choice for many dogs, resulting in fence destruction, damage to the dog's mouth and paws from the splinters, and, often, eventual escape. Additionally, if the wood is painted, the paint will be chewed off and ingested and can cause significant health problems. Likewise, if your dog is a digger and the wooden fence is placed over grass or dirt, your dog will dig himself an escape hole in no time. This is less likely if the wooden fence is over cement or a similar hard surface, but it is still fairly easy for a power digger to use his paws to pull the slats away from the fence posts and open up an escape hole.

Electrical fencing can be used either alone or in conjunction with a structural fence, and can be above ground or buried below. Both can offer excellent containment and are safe if used correctly. With an above-ground electrical fence, a charged electrical wire, called a "hotwire," is erected along the perimeter of your property. It emits a shock to any human or animal that touches it (think cattle fencing). Hotwires can function as the only type of fencing, as long as the wires are spaced close enough to each other horizontally to prevent an animal from ducking under or in between the wires.

The advantage of this type of electrical fence is that it keeps intruders and wildlife out as well as keeping your pets in. Hotwires are also excellent tools for augmenting existing fencing if you have a notorious escape artist in your family; strung along your fence line they can prevent your dog from climbing over, digging under, or chewing through your fence. This fence is not recommended for families with very young kids who might wander the yard and grab the wire accidentally. Please note that either type of electrical fence requires training the dog to understand it.

Flag boundaries

One way to help your dog understand the hotwire is to tie plastic ribbons, or "flags" to the wire when you first put it up. It's an easily recognizable visual cue so your dog can see the wire better and learn when he sees the flags that he does not want to get close. The advantage of taking this extra step is that your dog will think that whenever he sees those flags, there is a hotwire. This means that, with time, once your dog has a clear understanding and appreciation of the hotwire, you can attach the flags to regular wire or string along a perimeter and your dog will stay away, fully believing the line is a hotwire.

Does your dog tip toe through the tulips?

If your dog loves to run through and dig up a freshly planted flower bed, try planting seasonal color in hanging baskets. We always recommend running drip tubes to your baskets to help supplement hand watering.

▲ *Hedge rows of plantings can be used as an effective border, especially when hardy or thorny plants are selected. Closely planted hedge roses, such as the white flowering "Icebergs," make an attractive low maintenance barrier.*

▼ *A hedge of roses helps keep your dogs separated from your fence line.*

Planting hedges is an attractive way to improve the integrity of your fence, particularly with a non-solid fence (chain link, wrought iron, or wooden slats). The thick line of shrubbery will deter digging, jumping, scaling, chewing destruction, pacing, and fence fighting.

In hot, sunny yards, select drought tolerant hardy varieties like Euonymus and Juniper.

One of the most effective security borders to keep predators out, and your dogs in, is called "Pincushion Pine". The large shrub has a tall and slender growth habit making it a great screening and perimeter fence-line plant choice. The attractive foliage has small pine needle like leaves that are painful to touch for people and pets. New growth appears as a dusting of lighter green among a darker green foliage background.

Natal Plum

with its thorny disposition can help keep your dogs from fighting along a fence line. Dark green foliage offset with fragrant white flowers make a decorative addition to any garden. This hardy shrub can tolerate some K9 abuse and protect itself from too much damage with long thorns that grow along the stems and below flowers.

Foxtail fern

(Asparagus meyeri) is one of our favorites. Although puppies often find it entertaining to chew on the "tails," they rarely do enough damage to hinder the overall look of the plant. Small red berries in winter help feed visiting birds.

I need water!

Planting more delicate flowers in pre-cast concrete and clay planters is a great way to keep them out of dog harm's way, but what about watering? Sprinkler drip tubes are easy to install but the dogs can still get to them and they can be unsightly running up the side of a planter.

TRY THIS: Run your drip tubes up from the bottom of the pot and set your planter on "feet" to keep from pinching the tubes. This method keeps the garden looking tidy while protecting the drip tubing from your best friend's reach.

Garden Pathways

"Wayfinding" is the term for using garden pathways to encourage foot traffic to follow a predetermined path. Landscape designers use garden pathways to direct, or "wayfind," visitors through the garden. Pathways can be made from a variety of materials including flagstone, gravel, decomposed granite, mulch or concrete. Choosing the right material for your garden pathways follows the same rules as selecting non-living ground covers (Chapter 2). The idea is to direct and encourage foot traffic and flow through the garden along the path you choose.

Pathways should be 2-3 feet wide for single person walkways, what we refer to in the industry as "Duck Walks" because everybody needs to line up single file like a family of ducks to follow the path. This type of pathway works fine in smaller gardens where entertaining is kept at a minimum, but becomes a bottleneck when larger groups are visiting. If you routinely entertain groups of eight or more, size your pathways at 4-6 feet wide to accommodate two-way traffic. It's okay to vary the size and materials of different pathways in the garden. Entertaining yards need an entrance and an exit from each "outdoor room" area, or pathways large enough to handle two-way traffic, unless of course, you are designing for ducks.

▲ Narrow pathways force people to line-up like a family of ducks.

▲ *Damage from high foot traffic can be reduced by the using stepping stones.*

▼ *Lucy loves the feel of ground oyster shell covering Scott's Bocee court. This keeps her running across the court instead of tramping over his lush lawn.*

If you can't beat 'em, join 'em!

As pets travel through the garden they sometimes wear their own path. To reduce mud, remove turf from these areas and install pathways of gravel, decomposed granite, or mulch.

▲ Use decomposed granite pathways such as the is one to "wayfind" traffic through the yard

◄ Garden pathways are used to wayfind visitors to different outdoor rooms. In this photo, we are invited to walk along a rustic flagstone pathway, underneath a floral covered arbor to see what lies beyond. The mini-house actually serves as the dog house on this property. Lucky dogs!

Lawn and Order

Photo by Deidra Walpole

Which grasses make the best lawn for families with pets?

When choosing the best lawn variety, first select grasses that will thrive in your local environment and specific site conditions (sun, shade, etc.) From these choices, pick one that will best suit the needs of your whole family — children, adults and pets. The most important factor to consider in selecting a lawn grass is its ability to survive the intended use of the yard. The first consideration is sunlight. Is there adequate sunlight in the garden space to support shade-intolerant varieties? The second big consideration is whether the local climate favors cool-season or warm-season turf varieties. Next we look at the size, breed, and sex of the dog to help choose the right lawn. Sex? Yes, male and female dogs urinate differently in the garden. Male dogs typically will lift a leg and mark territory on a tree or fence post while female dogs will spot the lawn indiscriminately. We'll discuss more about training your dog to potty in the location you want, but for now let's just consider gender another factor in choosing the right lawn.

As an example, you might want to use a "tough" grass to accommodate a large, active female dog. The "toughest" grasses (considering only that characteristic) are the sports-turf grasses like Common Bermuda, Hybrid Bermuda, or Zoysia. These grasses have a trailing growth habit and handle heavy foot traffic better than cool season grasses (like Fescues). They also tend to fill in dog spots more quickly and they have a higher salt tolerance (urine).

Good choice right? Not so fast. These grasses grow very poorly in the shade. No matter how inherently tough these grasses are, they are simply unsuitable in shady areas. This is true whether the shade is due to trees, the sun's angle as seasons change, or compass location (north and east facing locations are cooler and more shaded than areas facing west or south). Furthermore, these varieties are only "tough" during their growing seasons, spring, summer, and fall…. they go dormant (turn brown and do not grow) during cooler winter months. When grasses are in a dormant state, dog traffic can quickly wear a muddy path through the turf thatch.

So, for sunny areas where winter dormancy is acceptable, the best lawns are warm-season turf varieties like Bermuda, Hybrid Bermuda, Kikuyu and Zoysias. These warm-season grasses are also deep rooting and drought-tolerant. The types of lawns that go dormant are also best for cold climate areas and can typically handle being snowbound. On the downside, because these grasses trail, plan on a little extra work every couple of years to "de-thatch" and keep your lawn well groomed.

Lush expanses of hardy tall fescue grass offer the benefits of drought tolerance and moderate foot traffic resistance

For sunny areas where year-round green is a must, consider hardy grasses like Tall Fescues and Dwarf Tall Fescues. These types of grasses are referred to as "cool-season" grasses and stay green year-round in temperate climates. They will die or go severely dormant in snowbound communities. Fescue grass varieties are primarily "clump" grasses and while they do "tiller" (spread wider) some, they do not actually trail. As such, they are appropriate for low to medium foot traffic with smaller to mid-sized dogs. The Fescues' non-trailing growth habit can often make maintenance easier because these lawns stay in the space for which they were intended and do not invade adjacent planters. Fescues are deep rooting and drought tolerant, but not salt tolerant so dog urine can burn spots. Fortunately, these unsightly spots are easy to seed and repair (see sidebar on how to repair a potty spot in next chapter).

Bluegrass is a cool-season grass that has a higher shade tolerance than Fescue. Bluegrass blends, over 100 cultivars, have a softer, finer blade and grow easily from seed or sod. This grass can actually fill in dog spots more quickly because it spreads by rhizomes (a horizontal underground stem that sends out its own roots and shoots) and tillers to create a dense sod lawn. Bluegrass, often called Kentucky Bluegrass, is a good choice for small to medium sized dogs and traffic.

Mixed lawns do better in mixed conditions! So, seed your lawn with mixed grass varieties like 15% Kentucky Bluegrass and 85% Dwarf Tall Fescue and you'll have a beautiful lawn than adapts better to semi-shade and dog traffic conditions. This lawn blend is good for small to large dog breeds in moderate climates.

Unfortunately, sod growers produce only the most popular varieties, which, except for a few, are mono-cultures. For sites with mixed conditions, planting your lawn with seed instead of sod may be your best bet, or even over-seeding an existing sod lawn can help it compete against foot traffic and adapt better to site conditions. For instance, if you add 15% Kentucky Bluegrass to a Fescue lawn, the Bluegrass, with its spreading growth behavior and improved shade tolerance, will help fill in foot traffic and dog spots.

The Bluegrass and Fescue blends help each other adapt to site conditions. Fescues are much more drought tolerant and deeper rooting than Bluegrass, but as the roots intertwine and grow together, the deeper Fescue roots actually bring water up to the Bluegrass through osmosis and improve its drought tolerance, resulting in a hardier turf blend.

Seed blends of different grasses naturally adapt to a changing environment, whether it be changes from sun to shade, hot to cool, wet to dry, or season to season. A good example of a high traffic blend is a "sports field" seed mixture containing a Bermuda and turf-type perennial Rye grass (tolerates shorter mowing heights).

Warm-season lawns are extremely hardy and repair faster from urine spotting, foot traffic and animal grazing. Most warm-season grasses don't grow from seed (referred to as stoloniferous), and must be planted by sod or hand planting stolons — small cuttings from growing shoots of the turf. These grasses, which include Common Bermuda, Hybrid Bermudas, Kikuyu, Zoysia, and St. Augustine, fill in damaged lawn areas by sending out runners from unaffected adjacent areas. Repairs take place rapidly during warm season months and sunny areas where these grasses rule. Growing in the sun, these grasses increase density when cut short, so they will do better where grazing animals like horses, rabbits, and turtles are a consideration.

Plant a mutt!

Just like mutts are often hardier than purebreds, lawns made up of mixed varieties can also improve hardiness. Most sites are a mix of conditions, so a suitable grass would logically be a "mix" of grass varieties.

Comparison chart of various grass types

Hot	**Common Bermuda**
Sunny	**Hybrid Bermuda**
Water Less Often	**Kikuyu**
Winter Dormancy	**Zoysia**
Grows Sideways	**St. Augustine**
Grows Upright	**Tall Fescue**
Green Year-Round	**Bluegrass**
Water More Often	**Turf-rye**
Shade	**Bentgrass**
Cool	

TOP 10 | LAWNS FOR YARDS WITH PETS

Photo by Southland Sod

TALL FESCUE

Tall Fescue

Best lawn for year-round green in sunny areas where drought tolerance is important. Good for small to medium sized dogs. Add 15% Kentucky Bluegrass to improve fill-in properties needed to handle foot traffic from larger dogs. Routine spot seeding required to maintain with dogs. Grows quicker than its cousin, Dwarf Tall Fescue.

Photo by Southland Sod

DWARF TALL FESCUE

Dwarf Tall Fescue

Tolerates a shorter mowing height and has a slightly finer blade than other Fescues, so it makes for a "well-groomed" lawn. Good lawn for year-round green in sunny areas where drought tolerance is important. Good for small to medium sized dogs, but it does grow more slowly than standard Tall Fescue. Add 15% Kentucky Bluegrass to improve fill-in properties needed to handle foot traffic from larger dogs. Routine spot seeding required to maintain with dogs.

DOUBLE-DWARF FESCUES

Double-Dwarf Fescues

The latest addition to the turf industry. While these true dwarf varieties are finer bladed and deep green in color, they grow too slowly for most petscaped yards. Extremely slow growth means less mowing for you, but very poor foot traffic recovery. Good for only very small to medium sized dogs. Consider gender here too. A small male dog would be great for this lawn, but a female that spots regularly will destroy it. Do not blend with other turf varieties. Routine spot seeding required to maintain with pets.

HYBRID BERMUDA

Hybrid Bermuda

Best lawn for heavy foot traffic, urine spot tolerance, and full hot sun. Trailing growth habit fills in high traffic pathways and urine spots rapidly during growing season. This is an excellent choice for colder climates because it goes dormant in winter months. Good for small to large dogs. Not suitable for shaded areas.

ST. AUGUSTINE

St. Augustine

Considered the best looking of the warm-season grasses, it has the highest shade tolerance. In fact, this lawn is a runner-type grass that does well in both sunny and shaded locations. This tropical grass is not especially hardy against foot traffic, but it does grow quickly enough to repair damage at a moderate speed. Good for small to large dogs during both the warm and cool seasons, if maintained at a taller height of 2 inches. Expect to hand weed this lawn as it is very sensitive to chemical weed controls.

KENTUCKY BLUEGRASS

Kentucky Bluegrass

Most common of the green year-round cool-season grasses. Shallow rooting means lots of watering. Good for sunny to semi-shade, but not great for hot full sun. Bluegrass trails from rhizomes and fills in damage from foot traffic and potty spots. Good for small to medium dogs. Add Perennial Rye to your seed blend for improved hardiness. Add Creeping Red Fescue seed for improved shade tolerance.

Photo by Southland Sod

PERENNIAL RYEGRASS

Perennial Ryegrass

Lighter green in color, this medium textured lawn does well in sunny locations. Fairly hardy against foot traffic and grows quickly from seed so potty spots can be remedied fairly quickly, but it does not self-repair. Expect to spot seed as part of your maintenance program. Good for small to large dogs. This seed mixes well with other similar varieties and is most often used as an ingredient in a mixed lawn for improved adaptability to site conditions.

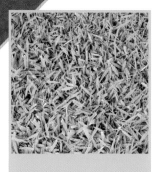

ZOYSIA GRASS

Zoysia grass

The hardiest of the warm-season lawns. Nearly bullet-proof against foot traffic in hot, sunny yards and extremely salt (urine) tolerant. Most pee-pee spots just turn a darker shade of green. Good drought tolerance. It is excellent for small to large dogs where winter dormancy is okay. This lawn has a tendency to build up thatch and requires annual dethatching as part of the maintenance program.

SEASHORE PASPALUM

Seashore Paspalum

As the name implies, Seashore Paspalum is best suited for hot, sunny, coastal climates where salt tolerance can be a problem for less hardy varieties. Coarse in texture, it is not a favorite for barefoot strolls through the garden. This warm-season lawn trails aggressively and fills in traffic and dog spots quickly. Weekly edging is required to keep it out of planter areas. Good for small to large dogs.

Photo by Southland Sod

CREEPING RED FESCUE

Creeping Red Fescue

This turf variety is great for transition zones adjacent to lawns or on small slopes. It does not have to be mowed and can be maintained as a rustic looking ground cover at 10-12 inches in height. Dogs like to graze on the taller shoots. Good for small to medium sized dogs in sun to partially shaded locations. This unique grass trails slowly from short rhizomes and handles light foot traffic when maintained tall and unmowed. It performs better when maintained at typical lawn heights. Creeping Red makes a good addition to seed blends for improved shade tolerance. Creeping Red Fescue is grown only from seed and not readily available as a sod.

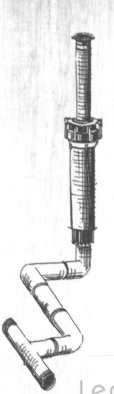

Less Broken Sprinkler Heads

Active dogs can create a nightmare for sprinkler systems. As dogs run through the garden they can knock into sprinkler risers and break the fittings and pipes below. Many home-owners have been frustrated by frequently broken sprinkler heads, lines and pipes from a rambunctious pet. Man's best friend or not, it can test a relationship for sure.

The simple solution is to modify your sprinkler installation method. We use a "swing elbow" configuration on our sprinkler system installations. Instead of mounting sprinkler heads directly into the top of the fitting, turn your fittings sideways and mount sprinklers on a series of threaded 90 degree elbow fittings. (See diagram for clarification.) Following a swing elbow sprinkler configuration will reduce your broken heads and make repairs easier if one gets broken by a pet. Instead of breaking the head, when a dog knocks into the head it will simply fall over, to be easily up righted by hand later.

Lawn Maintenance
Good maintenance practice promotes survival of lawns with pets

Some basic advice for healthy lawns.

Mow taller. Each added 1/4" of cutting height adds about 25% more leaf area to upright growing grasses. Leaf area is the key to a plant's ability to gather sunlight, produce carbohydrates, and grow deeper roots. Taller mowing leads to more "flesh" to support wear, more leaf to supply food (for grazing pets) and deeper roots to improve salt tolerance and more rapid recovery from urine damage.

Water deeper and less often. A general rule is to water the equivalent of an inch of rain, but only as often as necessary. The idea is to promote the healthiest, deepest rooting turf possible under given conditions. Watering deeper leaches salts (pet urine) beyond the root zone of tender new grass shoots. Watering less often promotes natural aeration and encourages bacterial activity which aids the decomposition of animal waste toxins.

Photo by Diana Harris

Water like rain. This term reflects the need (in clay soils) to irrigate "like rain," which is characteristically long and slow, an inch of rain occurring over several hours in a moderate storm. Typical pop-up spray-nozzle sprinkler heads used in residential landscaping apply an inch of water in only 20 minutes. That's the equivalent of a huge downpour or cloudburst! This often results in too much run-off as the lawn and soils in some communities don't absorb the water fast enough. To improve water penetration, try something pros, like golf course superintendents, use called "session irrigation," several shorter watering sessions one hour apart. The time between watering allows water to soak in deeper, encouraging deeper root growth and salt leach. Set your sprinkler timer to session irrigate until about an inch of water is achieved, but only water as often as necessary. Remember, allowing the soil to dry between watering helps aerate the soil and encourage healthy deep root growth.

Sprinklers are NOT chew toys! Protecting your sprinkler heads

A common problem caused by younger dogs is the chewing of wires attached to automatic sprinkler valves. Puppies are notorious for destroying any loose cables in the garden. To avoid this situation, protect your sprinkler valves with a faux rock or a sprinkler valve box. The same boxes that are used to protect sprinkler valves from vandals on commercial projects will keep out Fido too.

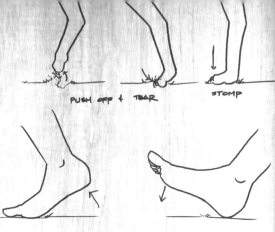

PUSH OFF & TEAR   STOMP

ROLLING MOTION; COMPRESS DIRT

Why "Foot Traffic" is a Problem

In the old classic "The Foot Book," Dr. Seuss tells us about all the different kinds of feet we meet … "small feet, big feet, here come pig feet." The fact is that feet and paws wear down turf differently. As people walk and run (can we include kids as people?) their weight rolls from heel to toe, causing mostly compaction problems. Dog paws, on the other hand (pun intended), actually dig in from the front claws, causing more tearing. To exacerbate the problem, dogs tend to pace and use the same pathways over and over again.

Soil compaction slows water penetration and can reduce root growth. To alleviate compaction, include "plug aeration" in your biannual maintenance practice. Plug aerator machines pull up "plugs" of soil, creating small holes that help water, air and fertilizer reach the root zone. To avoid damaging your sprinklers, be sure to flag your sprinkler heads before running this machine over your lawn.

The tearing nature of foot traffic from dogs requires routine seeding and topdressing combined with placing obstacles in the pathway to allow time for turf to heal. Use benches, patio furniture, or temporary fencing to redirect your pet's traffic pattern.

Plan to make repairs

Dogs will urinate, rabbits graze, cats will scratch, kids run and play. All of these activities can damage lawn areas. Prepare for and follow a systematic maintenance repair program to grow new plants to replace those abused and damaged plants. Professional football fields are over-seeded on a weekly schedule during playing season. Golf courses routinely fence off areas being reseeded or recovering from excessive wear. Let's follow the pros' example and keep a supply of seed and topdressing handy for regular repairs. Use seeding as part of a regular maintenance program, along with fertilization (6-8 times per year) and plug-aeration.

▲ *Keeping planters on the patio periphery allows plants to thrive without interference from rambunctious dogs.*

Burn Spot Solutions

How to properly spot seed a pee-pee spot: Repairing a dog pee-pee spot in 4 easy steps

1. **LEACH** out the salts (urea) by flooding the area with water. If you have clay soil and the water just sits on top, try adding a couple of drops of mild dishwashing liquid to a bucket of water and pour it slowly over the spot. The little bit of added soap acts as a wetting agent and will break the surface tension of water and help it soak deep into the soil.

2. **REMOVE** any dead turf and scarify (rough up) the soil to expose raw earth.

3. **APPLY** one handful of seed and work it into the top 1/4 inch of soil.

4. **TOPDRESS** the seed bed with mulch or loose, rich soil.

Most turf seeds take 7-10 days to germinate during growing season and need to be kept moist during this period. Expect to water 2-3 times per day for 7-10 days to ensure good seed germination. If you are seeding during a cooler time of year, use a little manure in your topdressing to add warmth and speed germination.

Causes of Lawn Damage

Seeing spots before your eyes? How can you tell if it is a dog pee-pee spot or something else? Brown spots in the lawn can be caused by a variety of factors such as insect damage, lawn fungus, poor sprinkler coverage or dog pee. Use this checklist to quickly identify the culprit before blaming your best friend.

seeing

Insect damage usually shows itself as a spreading brown patch where the grass in the middle pulls up easily. This is typically caused by root chewing insects like grubs and earwigs. Apply a pesticide to control these insects and keep your pets away from the area at least until it is completely dry. Be careful guys, men have a tendency to think that if a little is good, a lot will be better. Not true with pesticides, as it can be dangerous to over-apply. Always follow directions on the label. Repeat treatments may be required.

Lawn fungus often appears as "fairy rings," or 2-4 foot diameter large circular areas where grass can still be green in the center of the circle, but is surrounded by yellowing turf blades in circular patterns on the perimeter. The yellowing appears on the turf blade throughout and not just the tip. When you tear out a clump of grass it can smell like mildew. If you suspect you have a lawn fungus, visit your local nursery for the recommended "fungicide" to treat the problem. Check your sprinkler coverage too; often times fungus problems are brought on by drought-stressed conditions.

spots before your eyes?

Drought-stressed lawns, suffering from poor irrigation coverage, wilt from the top down. The tips of the blades will show signs of shrinkage or wilt before turning brown. An easy test for uniform sprinkler coverage on your lawn is to place coffee mugs in both the brown and green areas. Run your sprinkler system for about 15 minutes or so and check to see if the amount of water is the same in all the cups. This simple test will help you identify any sprinkler adjustments that may be necessary.

Dog pee-pee spots are usually brown in the center and surrounded by taller lush green turf. Dog urine contains urea, a form of ammonia, and is very high in nitrogen. While small amounts of urea are good (it is a component in most lawn fertilizers), a concentrated dose of this natural ingredient burns the spot in the center where it gets too much fertilizer, but turns the grass greener all around the area. You would get a similar effect if you poured a cup of fertilizer in just one spot.

Avoid spots all together by training your pet to urinate in a pre-planned area of the yard. There are detailed, easy-to-follow instructions at the end of this chapter for giving you total control over where your dog eliminates.

Lawn and Order

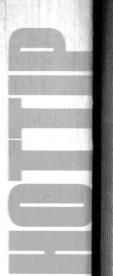

#1: The internal dilution solution

Keeping your dog well watered dilutes the concentration of urea in the urine and can help reduce the severity of pee-pee spots.

#2: The external dilution solution

Consistent and even watering will help to dilute the effects of the urine as well. To check sprinkler coverage, place coffee mugs on the ground in the area you want to check. Run your sprinkler system for about 15 minutes or so and check to see if the amount of water is the same in all the cups. This simple test will help you identify any sprinkler adjustments that may be necessary.

#3: The spur of the moment dilution solution

Until you've successfully trained your dog to pee elsewhere, if you catch your dog in the act, quickly dilute the urine with water from a garden hose.

"Potty Spot" Training

Teaching your dog to go in a specific place

You can minimize urine damage to your lawn and plants by training your dog to go potty in one specific area of your yard and not go on the rest of the landscaping. It's a simple strategy, but requires a few weeks of consistency on your part. As with many trained behaviors, it requires a two step plan where you simultaneously prevent puppy from peeing on the good grass while encouraging him to eliminate on the area you have chosen. This is MUCH easier to accomplish when a dog is first introduced to a yard, so if you're thinking about getting a new dog, or thinking about renovating your yard, you'll want to decide how you want to set up the potty spot and have everything in place before the dog is allowed in the yard for the first time.

A potty spot doesn't have to be huge; a 4x8 foot area is sufficient for one dog, though providing at least double that for two or more dogs is recommended. For guidance on choosing a ground cover, please read about the different varieties discussed in Chapters 2 and 3 and pick which one is best for you. If you have male dogs, remember that males tend to lift their legs and pee on a vertical item, whereas females like to squat and go right in the middle of a flat area. Males must have a tree, lamppost, or other vertical structure where it is okay for them to urinate, otherwise they can be quite unhappy. Make sure such a thing is provided in a yard or dog kennel if you do not want him peeing on his dog house, kennel wall, the table legs, chairs, etc.

Once the potty spot is ready for use, you can start training your dog to "go" there. This is as basic as it gets – simply lead the dog on leash to the spot every time you take him out for a potty break, don't let him leave the spot until he's eliminated, and praise him profusely when he goes. Some people like to reward with a treat as well as praise, though this is not necessary. Doggy will quickly get the message that going potty in this area makes owner very, very happy. Dogs like to please their owners, so your dog will begin to look forward not only to the relief of going potty, but the elaborate praise he receives by doing something so natural!

▲ *Side yards like these are perfect for specific potty spot training.*

Make sure your male dog has access to a tree, post, or other hardy vertical structure to keep him from peeing on valuable things in his yard. Here the coils of an air conditioning unit have been eaten away by repeated dog urine.

For this method to work, you need to deny your dog the opportunity to eliminate in any area other than the potty spot until he is fully trained. The above method automatically tackles this problem in part, because every time he is with you, on leash, at the designated potty spot, he is obviously being prevented from eliminating somewhere else. Any other time he is in the yard, however, you must watch him and be ready to correct him if he starts to go potty in an unapproved area. This means he cannot be allowed to roam around the non-potty areas of your yard without supervision until he is trained, which can take 8 to 12 weeks of consistent work until you can trust him. If you do spot him about to eliminate in an off-limit area, tell him "No!" sharply to stop his action, then get him over to the potty spot and proceed as above.

What if you have to leave him unattended in the yard sometimes before he has fully learned to use the potty spot? Then you will want to put up some sort of a barrier around the parts of the yard you are trying to protect. Depending on the size of your dog and how motivated he is to gain access to the off-limit areas, this can be as simple as surrounding the area with a decorative border, chicken wire, or puppy fencing. If your dog will jump over or plow through all of these suggestions and you don't want to erect sturdy permanent fencing around the off-limit areas, consider using a portable electric correction fence while your dog is in training. These are pricier than other options, but they are easy to use and highly effective, making it money well-spent. If you do choose the electric fence option, we recommend consulting a professional trainer to instruct you in proper use and safety guidelines.

Raccoon damage don't blame the pooch!

Not all lawn damage is caused by dogs. The damage in this photo was actually caused by several uninvited guests, raccoons. Wild raccoons will lift and "roll" back large patches of lawn area in search of grubs or worms to eat. They will also eat pond fish and aquatic plantings.

Beware of handling raccoon feces as it will often contain roundworm parasites that can be transmitted to humans and pets. Be sure to wear disposable gloves and dispose of feces promptly.

The best long term control of raccoons is to remove the food source. Treat lawn and planter areas with insecticides labeled for sub-surface insects like grubs and worms. If there is no food for the raccoons to eat, they will eventually move on. Animal traps are also available for rent from animal control services so you can capture the pests for relocation.

What to Put Underfoot

Ruby loves her strip of artificial turf, and it fits in perfectly with the garden landscape of her yard.

Ground Cover Alternatives to Lawns

Ground cover options other than grass

There are a number of hardy, decorative choices of living ground cover you can plant instead of or in addition to a lawn. Check with a nursery for recommendations of plants that grow well in your local climate and sun/shade conditions. If ground cover plants will be used as a potty area for dogs or cats, consider ease of removing solid waste from the plants. It is much harder to clean solid waste from thick vines than from low bushes and discreet, individual plants. The plants must also be able to tolerate being exposed to your dog's waste. Check with your local nursery or landscape professional for ground cover recommendations that are suited to your climate, and sun and shade conditions.

Nonliving ground cover
(wood chips, decomposed granite, gravel, river rocks, stonework)

Wood chips and mulch. Wood chips and other types of mulch can be an easy, affordable, and attractive way to provide ground cover in the yard and dog run. Mulch will compliment grassy or planted areas, giving a more "garden-like" appearance than concrete or granite. It stays cool and paw-safe even in moderate to high sun, and drainage is excellent. After the initial investment to cover the area, maintenance is relatively inexpensive, though it must be partially replenished every few months due to erosion and loss from cleaning up after the dog.

Important Safety Tip: No Cocoa Mulch! When choosing mulch, be sure to avoid cocoa-fiber mulch as it can be poisonous to dogs if ingested. In general, no type of wood chip or mulch is recommended for dogs who are obsessive chewers or like to eat anything they can fit in their mouths; the mulch material can accumulate in your dog's digestive system and cause significant health problems.

Gravel anchors the end of this Contemplation Garden, while providing excellent flooring material for a potty area. The bird bath attracts colorful wildlife to the window views. Photo by Deidra Walpole

Gravel and decomposed granite (DG). Gravel or Decomposed Granite (DG) is a highly recommended way to go for potty areas, high traffic areas, and even covering the majority of a dog run. Gravel and DG provide excellent drainage, it is easy to clean solid waste away and hose off urine, the small size of the individual rocks makes them gentle to your dog's paws, they stay relatively cool in moderate to high sun, and they are quite affordable to install and replenish.

Be mindful when planning your dog's area that many dogs do not like to lay down on gravel; therefore, avoid covering the entire area with this substrate. If it is used across the majority of the yard, make sure you provide a slab of concrete, turf, paving stones, or plain dirt so your dog has the option of relaxing on a softer surface. Though it is uncommon for dogs to eat the stones, gravel is not recommended for "Hoover dogs," those who swallow anything they can fit in their mouths. The stones can accumulate in the dog's stomach and intestines and cause significant distress.

River rocks. River rocks are larger, smooth, oblong rocks, measuring 2 to 3 inches on average. They are an easy and attractive option for providing a dog potty spot, but they have several downsides. Dogs often don't like the feel of the rocks and can be resistant to walking on them; training them to use the rocks may therefore be more difficult than with other types of ground cover. Likewise, river rocks should never be used to cover 100% of the dog's area as your dog may dislike walking around and lying down. Additionally, though they provide excellent drainage, their larger size and surface area cause them to get hotter and retain heat in direct sunlight more than their smaller counterparts (such as granite and DG). It is difficult to clean solid waste without including some of the rocks and they are expensive and inconvenient to replenish.

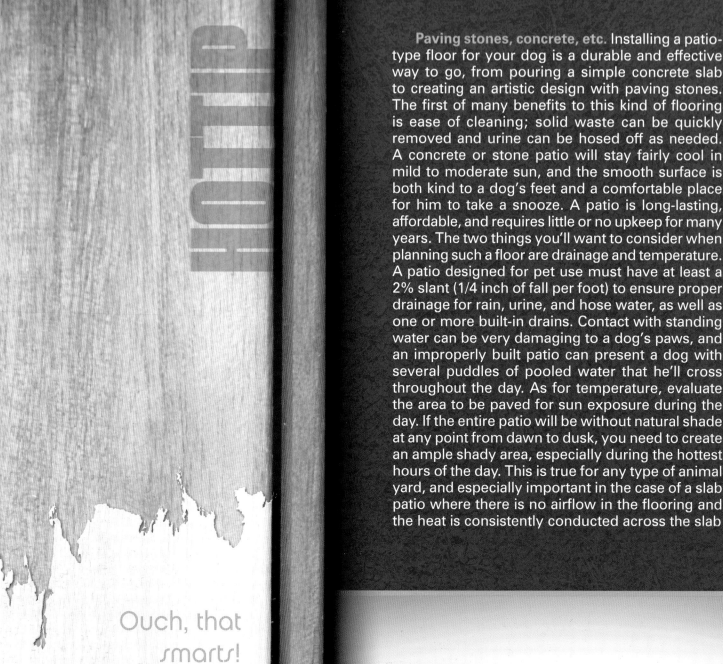

Paving stones, concrete, etc. Installing a patio-type floor for your dog is a durable and effective way to go, from pouring a simple concrete slab to creating an artistic design with paving stones. The first of many benefits to this kind of flooring is ease of cleaning; solid waste can be quickly removed and urine can be hosed off as needed. A concrete or stone patio will stay fairly cool in mild to moderate sun, and the smooth surface is both kind to a dog's feet and a comfortable place for him to take a snooze. A patio is long-lasting, affordable, and requires little or no upkeep for many years. The two things you'll want to consider when planning such a floor are drainage and temperature. A patio designed for pet use must have at least a 2% slant (1/4 inch of fall per foot) to ensure proper drainage for rain, urine, and hose water, as well as one or more built-in drains. Contact with standing water can be very damaging to a dog's paws, and an improperly built patio can present a dog with several puddles of pooled water that he'll cross throughout the day. As for temperature, evaluate the area to be paved for sun exposure during the day. If the entire patio will be without natural shade at any point from dawn to dusk, you need to create an ample shady area, especially during the hottest hours of the day. This is true for any type of animal yard, and especially important in the case of a slab patio where there is no airflow in the flooring and the heat is consistently conducted across the slab

Ouch, that smarts!

Smaller sized gravel can get caught between your dog's paws. This is especially true for dogs with long fur between their toes. Consider this when choosing your style of gravel.

Artificial turf. This is a good choice in many situations because dogs prefer going potty on grass over all other options, and artificial turf makes it possible without the grass dying. It stays cool in mild to moderate sun, it is easy to clean, and there are newer types designed specifically with pets in mind that are extra durable. A dog can differentiate between this and real grass, so it is easier to train it as a potty spot than training a dog to choose between two areas of real grass. Artificial turf is not recommended in yards where sun exposure is predominant and strong; the synthetic grass gets much hotter than real grass and can burn a dog's paws during the sunniest hours.

▲ *A faux turf putting green and fringe were the perfect solution for this yard with pervasive shade and heavy paw traffic.*

Providing for Pooch

Basic pet care considerations

This chapter covers customizing your yard in fun, creative, and attractive ways to accommodate man's best friend.

Glorious H2O

Water bowls, pools, fountains, ponds, and non-chlorine alternatives

A clean source of drinking water is of utmost importance for any animal. Your dog needs plenty of fresh water daily, especially in the hotter months. By fresh, ask yourself "Would I want to drink it?" If the answer is "No," you probably need to give your dog a new bowl of water! Dogs naturally drink enough water to maintain the proper balance for their bodies, so make sure you provide them more than enough at all times to account for variations in needs, evaporation, and other creatures drinking from the bowl as well. If your dog drinks more than two-thirds of the water provided throughout the day, you should increase the amount offered.

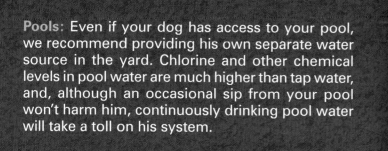

Pools: Even if your dog has access to your pool, we recommend providing his own separate water source in the yard. Chlorine and other chemical levels in pool water are much higher than tap water, and, although an occasional sip from your pool won't harm him, continuously drinking pool water will take a toll on his system.

Easy dog self-watering systems

A great way to ensure your dog can always get fresh water is by using an automatic watering nozzle. These attach to your water source and release water a few drops at a time when your dog licks it.

Fountains: Fountains can be a dog's water source if they are maintained with this in mind. As with other watering methods, the water in the fountain would need to be freshened daily, kept at an adequate level so the dog has plenty of water, and maintained without the use of harsh chemicals such as chlorine or bromine. Check with your local aquarium store for safe water-cleansing products.

Waterfalls and ponds: Waterfalls and ponds are a decorative way to add another water source in the garden for your pets. Pets can drink from the waterfalls themselves or from the edge of the pond. Be sure coping (pond edge) is stable so pets won't fall in. Proper pond design includes stepping the sides of the walls so pets can climb out if they go for an accidental swim. Stepped sides also aid in supporting a variety of aquatic plants. Bog plants are planted on the upper shelves at under 18 inches depth, while water lilies are submersed below 2-3 feet.

For water loving pets, be sure to install a larger pond basin and add extra gravel and rock protection for the liner since claws can puncture or tear the waterproof membrane if they choose to go for an active swim. See Chapter Nine for more on how to create your own beautiful backyard pond.

Dinner Time

What to consider when feeding the beast

Whether you are preparing a simple corner of the yard for your dog, or going all out on a deluxe doggy paradise, your dog or dogs will appreciate the extra effort of setting up an official feeding station for meal time. What does this mean? It means food and water bowls at appropriate heights for your dog's size. It means providing a stress-free mealtime routine and set-up for multiple dogs. And it means ease of feeding, cleaning, and food storage for you.

▲ *Several companies manufacture feeding stations that look like rocks and blend naturally into the garden. Photo by Rocktainer from Gamma2.*

First and foremost, a feeding station takes into account your dog's size. Putting a bowl of food or water down on the ground may be perfect for a Chihuahua, but as a dog's size goes up, the strain on his back and neck increases if he has to put his head all the way down into a bowl on the ground. There are a variety of companies that supply wooden or metal feeding stations which cater to your dog's size. This is especially important as a dog ages and his spine gets a little tighter.

Secondly, if you have more than one dog, be sure to create a routine to keep order during mealtime. This is extremely important, as dogs who would never fight in other situations can become competitive and aggressive when eating. Even if your dogs have never had a problem in the past, at any time they can suddenly start to grouch at each other if one tries to take the other's food. This can be avoided by separating them when feeding, a task that is easily accomplished if considered when planning the feeding stations. You can separate the dogs' bowls by space (place one feeding station at one part of the yard and the other several feet away), or by physical barrier (place one feeding station in a part of the kennel or yard that can be closed off from the other feeding station by a wall or fence). Alternatively, you can equip your feeding stations with short ties that clip onto your dog's collar and keep the dog close to the food bowl. This way you need only separate the feeding stations by a few feet while still preventing the dogs from crossing over to each other's bowls to steal or fight. The dogs are clipped to the stations until the food is eaten or they are clearly done eating. If there is still food left after 15 minutes, remove it and unclip the dogs.

When designing your yard, consider how and where you're going to store your pet food. Many feeding stations come equipped with food storage drawers, shelves, or bins. This makes feeding simplistic as the food is right there for easy access. Make sure you store the food in containers that will keep out not only your dogs but also rodents, raccoons, ants, and other insects. An additional time-saver is situating the feeding stations near your water source. Water should be changed at least once a day, and water bowls very near the water source tend to be kept cleaner and fresher than those far away. The food bowls should also be washed daily if canned or wet food is served, periodically if your dog only eats dry kibble.

Friendly advice for when Fido is filthy

How often will you be washing and grooming your dog? Some short haired breeds can go a month or two between baths, while other dogs need weekly bathing. Likewise, someone with a short-haired dog might not even own a dog brush, whereas the longer or curly-haired breeds need near daily brushing to keep their coats in top condition. If you own a breed with frequent grooming requirements, do think about adding a grooming station to your outdoor set-up. You and your dog will be equally pleased!

What should you consider when planning a grooming station? It needs to hook up to a water source, ideally with hot water as well as cold. It should be built with a platform adjusted for height such that when your dog stands on it, you do not have to bend over to wash or brush him. You need steps or a ramp for your dog to get up to the platform, unless he is small enough for you to lift him to it. You need a sturdy way to secure your dog on the platform and prevent him lunging off mid-bath. The grooming station should be designed with proper drainage in mind, taking into account the water will be soapy and full of hair and other solid debris. If your dog's fur requires a blow dry after a bath, make sure you include an electrical hook-up in your plan. Lastly, you'll want to include storage for shampoo, brushes, nail clippers, towels, a blow dryer, treats, etc., as well as a trash receptacle.

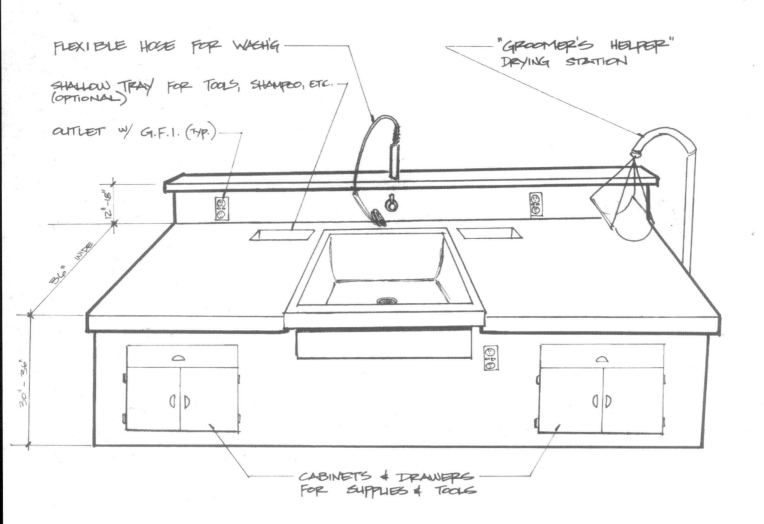

FLEXIBLE HOSE FOR WASH'G

SHALLOW TRAY FOR TOOLS, SHAMPOO, ETC. (OPTIONAL)

OUTLET W/ G.F.I. (TYP.)

"GROOMER'S HELPER" DRYING STATION

12" - 18"

36" WIDE

30" - 36"

CABINETS & DRAWERS FOR SUPPLIES & TOOLS

▲ *Consider ordering an extra ottoman for your cat or small dog and an extra lounge chair for your medium to large dog.*

◄ *Petscaping is a rapidly growing retail category, prompting creative design ideas like matching pet furniture or this doggy pool lounge. Photo by Frontgate Catalog.*

Lounging Around

Matching dog bed to patio furniture

Dogs and cats enjoy spending time with their owners, including lazily relaxing in the yard together. Having furniture specifically for your pets is a clever way to let them know they're wanted, while deterring them from the stuff that's not theirs. Today's patio furniture manufacturers are responding to the growing trend of "petscaping" by offering coordinated outdoor furniture designed for pets. When shopping for patio sets, ask if "pet specific" pieces are available.

In the Doghouse

Every dog should spend some time in his dog house.
This chapter describes your options for pet housing and refuge from the elements.

▼ *Cozy Cottage Luxury Dog Home from the Frontgate catalog (Cornerstone Brands, Inc.)*

Do you need a dog house (we're talking for your dog, not your husband)?

Just about every dog needs some sort of dog shelter or dog house in the yard. The only exception is if your dog is literally never left in the yard without you for more than five minutes, so there is no chance he will need shelter from the elements or a comfortable place to sleep. Dogs are descendants of wolves and have retained wolves' affinity for dens – cozy, warm, dry, dark caves where they can curl up and feel safe. Dogs love having a den box in the yard to call their own, even if they don't spend all their time outside.

How elaborate a dog house you need depends on the amount of time your dog will spend in it, what kind of weather it will endure, and how visible it will be in your yard. For a dog who is rarely out in the yard for very long, you can get by with a plastic crate tucked in the corner of your yard with its door propped open (or removed), just in case your dog

needs it. If your dog will frequently be out in the yard an hour or more each day, provide a house with solid walls to keep out wind, rain, and snow. Be sure to elevate your dog house to keep the interior dry, increase airflow, and facilitate clean-up. Ideally, the dog house walls would be insulated (a bonus in both cold and hot weather), though this feature is not crucial. Position the opening away from the prevailing wind. Lastly, if it will be clearly visible in the yard, consider coordinating the style of the dog house with the rest of your landscaping and furniture. Below are examples of dog houses, from the most basic shelters to extraordinary palaces for the truly pampered pooch. There are plenty of pre-fab styles available and do-it-yourself ideas online (check www.landscapingfordogs.info for tips and resources), so have fun and get creative while providing your dog his own private residence.

Photos by La Petite Maison

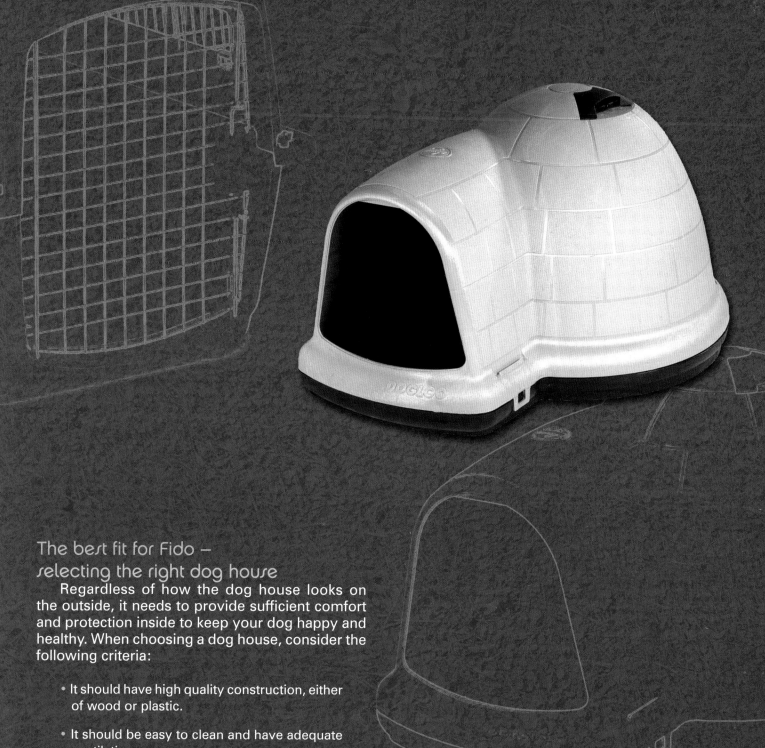

The best fit for Fido – selecting the right dog house

Regardless of how the dog house looks on the outside, it needs to provide sufficient comfort and protection inside to keep your dog happy and healthy. When choosing a dog house, consider the following criteria:

- It should have high quality construction, either of wood or plastic.

- It should be easy to clean and have adequate ventilation.

- If it is made of wood, check to ensure it does not splinter easily.

- If your dog is a habitual chewer, consider a rounded plastic dog house instead of a wooden house.

- Proper size means your dog can easily stand up in the house and comfortably lie down in it. However, bigger is not better in this case. Most dogs prefer a den box that is exactly big enough for them but not too big; they like to tuck themselves back into a cozy, tight space.

In placing your dog house, leave at least a six inch gap between the walls of the dog house and the walls or fence of your yard. This is so you can easily and frequently hose behind there, an area notoriously attractive to spiders, snakes, and other potentially dangerous pests. Increase comfort by placing blankets or pillows inside the dog house (as long as your dog doesn't ingest these items) as well as some toys. Remove these to hose out the dog house regularly – at least once a month.

A sloping side yard has been made into a functional yet attractive dry riverbed that serves as an easy-care dog run. The steps are made with treated timbers and Arizona flagstone. River pebbles make for clean paws and easy scooping while the sprinkler system keeps the area washed clean. The run is refreshed with additional pebbles about once a year. Willow has access from her own doggy-door located at the human stairs." Photo by Mary Barnhill

Dog runs and kennels

You may want to create a dog run (aka "kennel," or "dog yard") in your yard. This is a portion of your yard fenced off so that you have the option of containing your dog separate from the rest of the yard. It offers a place to put your dogs if you do not want them around your guests or when someone (pool man, gardener, etc.) is working in your yard. A dog run enables you to limit your dog's access to your main yard, which can reduce your dog's impact on delicate landscaping ,like a freshly-seeded lawn. In a family with multiple dogs, if there are any aggression issues between animals,

you can use a dog run to separate them to prevent fighting when they are in the yard unsupervised.

A dog run can range in size from a very large cage to a spacious sequestered area. Obviously, the more time the dog will be spending in it, the bigger it should be, so he has adequate room to move around. Regardless of size, it needs to have the same basic features discussed previously – shelter from the elements, a den box, a potty spot, and an area for food and water bowls. If it will be used to separate fighters, choose proper fencing to prevent interaction through the fence (Chapter 1).

▲ *Patio covers like this provide a shady spot for you and your pets to escape a baking sun.*

◄ *A deluxe dog bed like this is a simple and comfortable way to provide a shady spot. Photo by Frontgate Catalog.*

Made in the Shade

Heat relief with trees, tarps, and misting systems

Shade is an important consideration when designing your garden for pets. Heat-stroke is a common problem with pets left outdoors to fend for themselves. Pets can become ill or even die in a very short period of time from heat stress. Providing lots of water is just not enough, ample shade must also be available to keep your pets healthy. Use a combination of trees, plantings, tarps and mist systems to keep your pet cool and comfortable year-round.

Trees & Plantings

Properly placed trees in the garden add beauty, provide shade from the sun and shelter from wind, and add value to your home. Trees can also help control heating and cooling costs. For instance, placement of deciduous trees (those which lose their leaves in winter) on the south and west sides of the home will provide shade in summer and still allow sunlight and warmth through during the winter months when they are leafless.

Fruit bearing trees provide food and shade, but beware of some pit fruit varieties such as Apricot, Cherry, and Peach, whose pits are toxic to dogs; fallen fruit becomes a big safety hazard.

A Doggy Sundial?

Can you tell what time of day it is by observing your dog's napping routine? Most dogs love to bask in the warmth of a patch of sunshine. You have probably noticed your dog adjusting his snooze spot as the sun travels across the sky. Eventually you may be able to estimate the time of day based on his location in your yard!

Shade Canopies

Shade sails are a cost-conscious option for adding shade to any garden or dog run area. The lightweight canvas covers are available in a variety of colors to coordinate with your outdoor furnishings. The shades are inexpensive and easy to install, so consider using several in the yard. Companies like "Coolaroo" offer various geometric shapes from which to choose. Beware when using these products in windy areas; shaped like sails, they can create a tremendous pull (called wind shear value) and damage structures when improperly attached. Choose a strong fence, post, or tree to secure the corners of the shade.

▼ *Photo by Coolaroo Catalog*

Mother Nature's misters

When people sweat or perspire it cools their skin as the water evaporates. Just as people perspire, trees and plantings "transpire," meaning that evaporating moisture from the surface of the leaves cools the tree. As a result it can be 15 degrees cooler under the canopy of a shade tree compared with being under a solid roof cover… nature's own misting system!

Pups love a pupsicle!

Top three ideas to keep pets cool in the summer:

#1: Store treats in the freezer.

Dogs like to lick frozen cubes made from low sodium chicken or beef broth. Freeze a rawhide bone in the center and you've made a Pupsicle!

#2: Set up an above-ground kiddie pool

for pets that like to swim. Change water frequently and avoid adding chlorine.

#3: Add ice cubes to the watering bowls.

Mist Systems

In areas where summer temperatures can be stifling it is a good idea to invest in a mist system. Misters can be placed around patio and dog run areas and connected to a standard garden hose or even connected to a sprinkler timer control valve and run automatically during the hottest part of the day. Most pet stores now carry easy-to-install low pressure mists systems perfect for residential gardens.

Pool Fencing/Safety/Ramps

It is estimated that thousands of dogs drown each year in residential swimming pools. The problem is that many animals can find their way into a pool, but then can't find their way out. Dogs do not have great depth perception and, if they're not regular swimmers, often panic and drown. If you have a pool, a spa, or a sizable pond in your yard, it is recommended you provide a way for

▼ *Collector basins on vanishing edge pools can be a safety hazard for pets. Be sure to include steps or a Scamper Ramp on lower basin.*

Control digging by adding more shade

Dogs instinctively dig to get down to the moist soil to cool themselves when over-heated. Control digging by adding more shade options in the garden.

*Scamper Ramp
by Gamma2.*

your dogs (or other pets and wild animals) to easily get themselves out should they choose to enter or accidentally fall in. The built-in steps of a pool are often adequate for large dogs, but even the top step can be too deep to aid a small or medium-sized dog. Likewise, spas rarely have dog-friendly steps, and not all ponds have a gradual slope for an animal to climb. In any of these cases an animal can easily drown trying to exit the water, even if it is a skilled swimmer. Consider adding a ramp of some type to protect your animals from having a frantic and tragic experience.

Make it easy to exit the pool

Swimming pool owners may want to consider the installation of a "Skamper Ramp" to provide an easy water escape route for home pets and visiting critters. The ramps install easily onto the side of your swimming pool or pond and can prevent accidental drowning.

*Scamper Ramp
by Gamma2.*

It is estimated that
THOUSANDS
of dogs drown
each year in
residential
swimming pools.

Training your dog an exit strategy:

Once you have determined there is a reasonable way out of the water or added a ramp if there wasn't, you'll want to train your dog how to swim to the exit and get himself out. Contrary to common belief, not all dogs are naturally good swimmers, and many need a supervised chance to practice before they are water-safe. Resist the urge to toss your dog in the deep end and hope for the best! Instead, try coaxing him in with praise and treats and a little bit of physical encouragement if he'll tolerate it. This works best with a pair of trainers, one with him out of the pool urging him towards the one in the pool with the treats. Once he's in the water, guide him to the escape route and help him find it if he gets confused or frantic. Make sure to praise him for his efforts once he gets himself out. Repeat this process several times over several days each swim season, even if your pet does not enjoy the experience, until he can deftly exit the water. This basic training exercise could save your pet's life.

Game On!

Dog Training 101

Some "basic" concepts
from Carolyn Doherty

There are training tips throughout this book for initiating, sculpting, and improving your dog's behavior. It is necessary, therefore, to first discuss the general importance of dog training and explain key concepts so you have the knowledge to work with your dog correctly.

Why training is important.

I am always surprised when I hear a dog owner say, "My dog doesn't need any training because he's just going to be a pet." Training your dog to respond to basic commands gives you a way of communicating with him; it's the start of simple language. Most dogs are capable of learning at least 100 distinct commands! Few dogs are ever taught that many, but the "basic" commands are a must to facilitate an excellent dog-and-owner relationship.

There are three vital advantages gained through basic obedience training:

- You establish authority over your dog

- You develop a collaborative process of communication with him

- You teach him functional commands that will help you to shape his ideal behavior within your life.

Basic obedience commands traditionally include sit, down, stay, short distance or on-leash come, and walk on a leash. These are optimally learned through a group obedience class, which you will find offered many places, including county parks, pet stores, and private lessons. I recommend enrolling any newly acquired dog in one of these classes, whether a puppy or an adult, because the dog will learn to focus on you with distractions. A group class has the added, invaluable bonus of socializing your dog around people and other dogs. This book will expand on those basics with instructions for speak, quiet, leave it, off-leash recall, go say hi, find it, and fetch it.

How to train —
Rewards, timing, and baby steps.

Teaching a dog a command is an extremely straightforward procedure, but if you've never done it before (or have never done it well before), it can feel as confusing and frustrating as the foreign language it truly is. So let's start with a discussion of dog training in general. Dogs do not understand English (or any language), but they are capable of linking an auditory or visual signal with a behavior. This is a really important concept, because it means it is up to you to help your dog link the word "sit," for example, with the action of sitting down. To be successful at this you must use your intelligence and patience to communicate what you want, and be willing to adjust your method if it's not working. Dogs are inherently driven to please their owners,

Halt before you hit
Punishment is not effective training!

Many novice dog owners try to use "Positive Punishment," (often erroneously referred to as "Negative Reinforcement") to train their dogs basic commands. Common examples of this are rubbing a dog's nose in a housebreaking error, yelling a command louder if it's not done the first time, and hitting a puppy after he chews up a favorite shoe. These methods have been passed down through the generations, but they don't teach your dog anything constructive. If your dog looks "sorry" after such a correction, it's because he's wary of your harsh tone, not because he knows he did something wrong and is feeling guilty. Ignore mistakes as much as possible, and look harder for opportunities to create and praise successes. Save corrections for behaviors that, when caught, absolutely must be stopped that moment, such as growling at a child or catching your dog in the act of peeing on the rug.

so whenever your dog behaves contrary to your wishes, instead of thinking he's being "stubborn," or "bad," or "obstinate," think to yourself, "I have not clearly communicated what I want yet, so I need to come up with a better way of teaching him this."

Rewards: Successful training comes from "Positive Reinforcement," which means giving the dog some type of reward (praise, petting, a treat, etc.) when he does what you want, so he wants to do it again. Unless your dog is actively doing something harmful, aggressive, or destructive, there is no need to train with punishments such as verbal corrections, slip chain corrections, hitting, grabbing, or otherwise manhandling the dog; training is all about teaching the dog what you want him to do, not making him pay for his mistakes until he figures it out.

Timing: The clearer you are about what you're rewarding, the faster your dog will learn the command. Try to reward your dog the very second he does what you want, so he can make that mental connection. If you're training a "sit," say "Good Boy!" the moment he sits, and don't tell him "No" if he immediately gets back up. If you wait until your dog has stayed seated for several seconds and then say "Good!" it is unclear if you are rewarding the action of sitting or the action of staying put.

Baby Steps: Lastly, when training something new, break it down into small steps and solidly train the first step before trying to add the second. In the example above, I mentioned you should not expect a "sit-stay" when first training a "sit." However, if you want to train your dog to automatically stay put after you ask him to sit, and not get up until you release him, that's great — just break it down into baby steps. Once you've trained "sit" and your dog does it consistently when asked, you can add the requirement of him staying there for two seconds until you say a release word. Then once this is consistent, you can elongate the time he is required to sit by gradually increasing the duration before the release word. By breaking behaviors into easy-to-train steps, you increase your dog's confidence and success while decreasing your frustration!

Your dog makes an enthusiastic workout partner

Outdoor Activities with Your Dog

Your dog makes an enthusiastic workout partner — he'll never try to weasel out of exercising, and he won't keep you waiting while he changes into his gym fur! Walking, running and just plain horsing around are always fun and no special equipment is needed, although plenty is available.

Dog parks are popping up all over the country. Creating your own at home dog park is a fun and easy way to keep your family and dogs entertained. Here is a list of games you can play with your dog to take your exercise activity to another level.

Teaching a "Fetch"

A trained retrieve, or "fetch," is a great behavior to teach any dog. Most dogs will enjoy fetching, so you need not have a retriever to have hours of fun with your dog chasing a ball, toy, or flying disc. That said, all dogs (even retrievers) need to be taught exactly how you want the game to go. A few simple training sessions will have your dog happily bringing back the item you throw over and over, instead of playing "keep away" (wherein he goes after toy, grabs it, runs in the other direction, and you spend the rest of the afternoon chasing after him to get it back!). Below are step by step instructions for teaching a fetch. For best results, begin the process indoors, with very few distractions around. Once your dog is consistently bringing back the toy, move the training outdoors.

STEP 1: Teaching the "Fetch it" command

Get doggy excited by whatever item you want him to fetch. If your dog is naturally excited by tennis balls…great. If not, teach a fetch with a toy he likes better, perhaps a stuffed squeaky or a rope toy. Entice your dog to put it in his mouth by waving it around, shaking it at him, holding it out to him, or baiting it with a little bit of peanut butter. As your dog grasps the toy say "Fetch it" and then praise and reward dog. If he is reluctant, start small by rewarding your dog for even sniffing or touching the toy with his muzzle, then encourage up to taking it in his mouth.

STEP 2: Teaching the "Give" command

Now that doggy is eager to grab the toy, he needs to learn to "give" the toy back. Continue to praise him for taking the toy when you say "Fetch it," but now say "Give" after he's had it in his mouth for a few seconds. This is most easily accomplished if you present a treat right after the command, as he will naturally drop the toy to take the treat. Praise him immediately. If he is unwilling to relinquish the toy or if he runs away holding the toy, attach a short leash to his collar and ask again. If you hold him near you with the leash he will eventually drop the toy so you can praise him. Resist the temptation to chase after him – that's what teaches Keep Away instead of Fetch!

Once you have refined the "Fetch it" and "Give" commands, developing a game of Fetch is elementary. Simply show the toy to your dog and get him excited about it, then toss it a short distance and say "Fetch it!" Once he has it, call him to you and say "Give." As he masters this idea, you can toss the toy farther and farther. As in Step 2, if he fetches the toy and then runs away from you with it, attach a long leash or line to his collar so you can correct him by bringing him back to you and saying "Give." Taught this way, there is no need to include teaching him a "Bring it" command or call him to you each time he gets the toy, as that step is built into the "Fetch it" command. When you are done with a session, put the toy away where your dog cannot get it. This will increase his enthusiasm for it next time and he will look forward to your Fetch sessions.

Do	Don't
Allow your dog several sessions to master this game	Try to teach more than one step at a time
Start training indoors with low distractions	Get frustrated by your dog's distractibility when you first go outdoors
Have fun during your training sessions and then stop while it's still fun for both of you	Continue the session if your dog is tired or disinterested
Make sure your dog's teeth are healthy and able to firmly grab a toy before starting	Begin training with a large, awkwardly shaped, or heavy toy that is hard for your dog to hold (although you can increase difficulty once your dog is a pro at the simple stuff)
Praise your dog throughout the process for every right move he makes	Allow your dog to keep the toy at the end of the session

Game On!

Dog-friendly flying discs

Pet suppliers make special discs made with light, flexible cloth in the middle and a padded rigid outer ring for stability. These are much easier for dogs to pick up than the standard, hard plastic variety.

Teaching a dog to catch a ball or a flying disc in the air

If you have an athletic dog who you think would enjoy jumping up to catch a ball or flying disc in the air, training this impressive trick is pretty easy. Start with the three basic steps to teaching a "Fetch," as outlined above. Even if your dog has a solid "Fetch it" with a ball or soft toy, you will want to spend some time introducing a flying disc, as its shape and rigid structure can be unappealing to a dog at first. If your dog seems scared or adverse to the flying disc, try feeding him or offering him water from the disc for a few days before turning it into a toy. Then follow these additional simple steps for extra-active fun!

STEP 4: Teaching a dog to catch something in the air

Have you ever tossed a peanut into the air and caught it in your mouth? Can you catch it if someone else tosses it? Think back to how much you practiced to perfect this party trick! Most dogs can catch something in the air, but just like you, they have to learn the skill. Put your dog in a sitting or standing stay, then say "Fetch it" as you gently toss a treat to him underhanded, with a big arc so he can easily see and track it. If he catches it, praise verbally (he'll also get a food treat by default!). If he misses it, whether it was his fault or a bad throw, don't let him have the treat. Grab it from the ground before he can. If he has a solid "Stay," this shouldn't be a problem, but if you need help preventing him from grabbing the treat off the ground, have him on a leash when you do this and if he misses the treat hold it taut until you can pick it up. Toss it again until he is able to catch it in midair. Practice this with him over and over until he is an expert air-catcher.

STEP 5: Transferring to a toy, ball, or Frisbee®

To transition from a treat to a toy, start by saying "Fetch it" and tossing the toy to your dog from a short distance. Just like with the treat, allow him to have the toy and get praised only if he catches it in the air. Increase distance as he masters catching, until you are up to 10-15 foot tosses. Now you can begin having him chase after the toy instead of it coming right to him. Make sure he isn't in a "Stay," as you want him to move to chase the item! Toss it to him, but aim a couple of feet to the side of him and say an enthusiastic "Fetch it!" as you throw. If he catches it, go crazy with praise. If he misses, don't reward him for picking it up from the ground. Toss the toy right to him again to remind him of what you want, then follow up with a toss that's just a couple of feet to the side of him. ***BE PATIENT!*** This step can take longer than any of the others, so keep at it and keep it positive. He'll get the concept eventually and before you know it, your dog will be doing some impressive outdoor acrobatics.

Teaching a dog to play "Hidden Treasures"

Hidden Treasures is another game your dog will love, and it's great because you can either play it with her or set it up to entertain her when you are gone. It involves teaching the "Go Find It" command, then putting things in your yard for her to find. It's important to note that this game will encourage your dog to dig if you bury the "treasure." If you have concerns about this, play this game by only hiding treasure above ground. If you will include burying the "treasure," consider designating a portion of your yard for this purpose and train your dog to only play the game there.

STEP 1: Teaching the "Go Find It" command

Begin by taking a treat and letting your dog see you "hide" it somewhere. This can mean burying it under a shallow pile of sand in a sandbox, sticking it behind a rock, placing it under a pile of toys, etc. Show her the treat first and get her excited about it. Have her on a leash and stop her from getting the treat until you give her permission. When ready, tell her "Go Find It!" and allow her to get the treat. If she is confused as to where it is, lead her to it and help her find it while repeating the command. Praise her when she finds it and let her eat it. Don't bury the treat too deep (just a couple of inches) until she gets the idea.

Game On!

If this sight seems all too familiar to you, creating a digging spot and teaching "Hidden Treasures" can save your yard while satisfying your digger.

Clever digging control

The Hidden Treasure game is great for dogs with a digging problem who are destroying your yard. Follow the instructions in Chapter 7 about setting up a special digging spot, then use this game to make the training extra fun!

STEP 2:   Playing the game

Once your dog understands that "Go Find It" means there is something desirable hidden somewhere in the yard, you can turn it into a game. Now you can hide the treasure when she's not looking, so she needs to use her intellect and special traits to find it. Be creative and look for ways to integrate her specific abilities. Hound dogs have a super keen sense of smell, so you can hide treasure pretty deep in sand or in far corners of your yard to keep her working for her treats. Terriers are crafty hunters and skilled diggers who specialize in furrowing out game; challenge yours by hiding treats beneath a tower of small stones, on a tree branch where she'll need to stand on her hind legs to get it, or in a bin of toys so she'll have to dig through the box to find the treat. Cheer her on with verbal praise and repeating the command as she works to find all her treasure, and give her lots of praise and love once she's found all the treats.

Once she has the hang of this game, she can play it by herself when she's outside alone. Hide the treasure before you put her out, then tell her "Go Find It!" before you leave the yard. She will enjoy trying to find all the surprises you've left for her. Without you there to coach her, how will she know when she's found them all? She won't, and may either quit before she's found them all, or continue looking after she's found them all. Neither scenario is bad, though never hide raw meat as treasure or anything else that is subject to rapid spoiling so that if she misses some treasure it won't make her sick if she finds it later.

This is not a good game for multiple dogs to play at the same time! Even dogs that normally get along well can get competitive and aggressive towards each other if they're running around looking for hidden treats. If you have more than one dog, sequester one in a separate area while you play the game with the other in the yard, then bury more and switch.

Other forms of entertainment

Another thing you can do to help combat your dog's boredom when he's in the yard is to leave "doggy puzzles" for him to solve. Several companies make sturdy toys specifically designed to be filled with peanut butter or treats. Your dog will spend hours getting those treats out, and not even notice that you are gone! Some dogs love to play with ice cubes, so dump a bunch in his water bowl or on the ground for him to fish out and crunch while he's out there. For extra amusement, try freezing treats or a rawhide bone in a small bowl of water, remove the block from the bowl, and then place it outside with him as you leave for the day. For added flavor, use low sodium chicken or beef broth instead of water.

Agility: A Creative Solution to Backyard Boredom

Agility is a competitive canine sport that has gained tremendous popularity recently. It involves training the dog to run an obstacle course, with guidance from his handler, as quickly and skillfully as possible. These courses include a variety of athletic challenges, such as jumps of various sizes, climbing obstacles, weave poles, tunnels, and a pause table.

The dog must use aerobic endurance, anaerobic strength, and brainpower to master the obstacles, making agility training an ideal solution for exercise needs and battling boredom. But you need not be competition-bound to reap the benefits of agility; you can enjoy this hobby at home with some equipment pieces and a little training instruction (you can learn the techniques from agility books, beginning agility group classes, or hiring a trainer).

Training a dog to run a course is different than training basic obedience, and will be a stimulating learning experience for both you the trainer and your pooch. It's a great option for outdoor bonding and exercise when you want a break from walks or playing fetch. Wear your running shoes and be prepared to get some exercise yourself, as you'll need to be actively working right there alongside your dog!

You can put together a course in your yard consisting of just one or two obstacles, and build on length and complexity as you and your dog get the hang of it. There are numerous online sources of affordable agility equipment, as well as websites with instructions for creating your own. For example, we've detailed the simple process of making a bar jump below.

Game On!

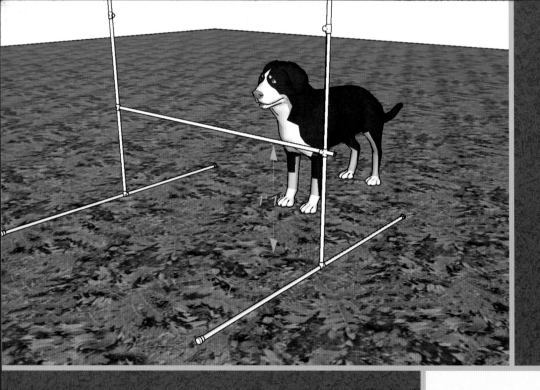

Here is an easy to build project (or buy it on line for about $50). This clever contraption can be made at home with a couple of foam noodles and some PVC pipe.

Topiary touches:
Fun landscaping accents

Introduce a little fun and whimsy to your *Petscaped* garden with topiary animals. These pre-wired cages are reminiscent of Disney's "It's a Small World" ride, and will bring a smile to all your garden visitors.

Amusing topiaries are available in shapes to match almost any pet. These photos are from www.showdogtopiaries.com, a site dedicated to garden art that mimics show dogs. You can purchase wire cages, plant them up in the garden and wait for them to fill in, or you can buy ready-stuffed moss statuary.

▶ Use a topiary fire hydrant to identify the area that you set aside in the garden as the pee-pee spot.

Dog-gone it!

Common Garden Behavioral Issues

Easy solutions for common outdoor problems

Nobody is perfect, and this applies to your dog as well! Some of the most common complaints from dog owners involve things the dog is doing in his yard. These can be particularly dangerous or troublesome because they lead to serious results such as escape, attacks, costly destruction, and disharmony with neighbors. This chapter focuses on training techniques you can do to solve common bad behaviors in the garden. Before trying these solutions, make sure you understand the training guide in Chapter 5.

Barking

Is your dog driving you or your neighbors crazy?

If your dog barks all day long while locked in the dog run or has sporadic bouts of barking you can't control, you need to change this behavior before you go crazy or the neighbors vote you out of the neighborhood! For immediate relief, a citronella oil anti-bark collar can be a safe and simple solution, but be wary of anti-bark collars. A popular type uses a shock collar that respond to a dog's barking by emitting a small electric charge. Use caution with these and, ideally, have a professional trainer instruct you on proper technique; used incorrectly these collars can exacerbate the problem, damage your relationship with your dog, and even cause physical harm. If the barking problem only occurs in one discreet location (such as in a dog run), consider installing a sound-activated overhead high pressure water spray system to distract the dog from barking. The water will come on automatically in response to barking with a powerful spray that will deter your dog from continuing to make noise.

One of the most clever and effective ways to curb incessant barking is to teach your dog to "Speak," or bark, on cue, and the "Quiet" command to get him to stop. Most dog owners try to teach a "Quiet" or similar command without also teaching the "Speak." You will get much better results if you teach both. It may sound crazy and counter-intuitive to teach a dog with a barking problem to bark more, but only until you understand that barking is your dog's way of communicating. Expecting a frequent barker to remain completely quiet all day, every day, is akin to telling a chatty person to stop talking indefinitely — eventually that person is going to explode with conversation. This is what your dog is doing in your yard when you are gone, because he's learned it's the time he can bark without correction. But if you teach your dog to speak, and ask for it several times a day, and praise him for doing it when you ask, and praise him for stopping when you ask, you change the dynamic. As with any trained command, you increase your authority over your dog and improve your relationship with your dog by adding to his command vocabulary. And more importantly, you give him a chance to be heard, to exercise his vocal chords, to get praised for talking to you, and to learn there is a proper time for barking. He will be far more accepting when you tell him "Quiet" out in the yard if he's already spoken with you that day!

Digging

When your dog does unauthorized excavation

Dogs love to dig — they get relief from the heat, it's something to do when they're bored, and it's great exercise. It's also devastating when your loyal pooch destroys your flower bed or systematically digs up an entire lawn. If you have a "digger," the solution to this problem is twofold: deter the dog from digging where he shouldn't, and encourage the dog to dig where he should.

"I'm just not digging it!" — Reduce his desire to dig

There are several things you can do to reduce his desire to dig. For one, keep his nails very short. This helps in two ways — your dog will feel less of an urge to wear them down and it will be less enjoyable for him to dig if the nails are trimmed close to the quick (as the nails will be more sensitive). You can trim the nails with traditional dog nail clippers or get fancy by using a sanding head on a Dremel (Please consult your vet or groomer first for instruction on how to safely Dremel a dog's nails as this can be dangerous and stressful if done incorrectly).

Secondly, never let him watch you dig or garden. You are his hero and he wants to be just like you; when he watches you working in the garden he gets ideas about how to emulate you. When he's not watching, fill the holes with something unpleasant

Tied to a tree, Chief readily barks to let Carolyn know he'd like to join her. Once he starts barking, she encourages him by saying 'Good Speak' and giving a visual cue.

Then Carolyn steps in with a food reward, too, so Chief understands quickly that he is being asked to bark.

Speak and Quiet

To train "Speak," you need to first identify things that get your dog to bark. Common triggers are seeing another dog or other type of animal, being restrained from getting to his owner, trying to get at a treat, being enticed with a favorite toy, hearing the doorbell, and seeing water spraying from a hose. If your dog tends to bark at any of these triggers, or something else you've identified that you can recreate, you can use it to get him barking. First restrain him on a 6-foot leash in a fixed location, such as tied to a tree or table leg. This is so you can control his position, as he is going to want access to whatever is making him bark (this alone may be an effective trigger, since, when tied, many dogs will bark to their owners if the owner starts to walk away). Every time he barks at the trigger, tell him "Speak!" and pay him with a small treat. Once he starts barking, the excitement of your encouragement and treats will keep him barking until you end the session. At first you'll be saying "Speak" after he barks, so it will go "Woof" — "Speak!" — pay with a treat, "Woof" — "Speak!" — pay with a treat. Once he figures out you're paying him for barking, begin paying only for barks that come after the cue, so you switch to "Speak!" — "Woof" — pay with a treat, "Speak!" — "Woof" — pay with a treat. Training generally goes very quickly once you find a good trigger. Within a 3-4 sessions you should be able to remove the trigger and get a bark in response to saying "Speak!"

Once you can easily get your dog to bark, you are ready to get him to stop! Use the command "Quiet" to let him know when the barking must end. You just need a way to distract him from barking long enough to reward the moment of quiet, such as showing him a treat, a favorite toy, ringing a bell, tossing and catching your keys, etc. Say "Quiet!" then do the distraction. When he stops barking to focus on the distraction, say "Good Quiet" and pay him a treat. Soon he'll learn he's getting a treat for barking and for not barking, and this will make him very happy! Remember, no punishments; simply don't pay the "speak" until he barks, and don't pay the "quiet" until he stops. Once these commands are trained, you should ask him to speak a few times every day so he gets his barking out of his system.

Training a dog to dig in a specific spot

Begin by taking a treat and letting your dog see you bury it in your designated spot. Show her the treat first and get her excited about it. Have her on a leash and stop her from getting the treat until you give her permission. When ready, tell her "Go Find It!" and allow her to get the treat. If she is confused as to where it is, lead her to it and help her find it while repeating the command. Praise her when she finds it and let her eat it. Once she has the hang of this game, she can play it by herself when she's outside alone while satisfying her need to dig. Hide the treasure before you put her out, then tell her "Go Find It!" before you leave the yard.

to dig up because dogs often return to a hole over and over. You can get fancy by placing lava rocks in the holes and covering with a light layer of dirt; the texture of the lava feels weird to their paws (think nails on a chalkboard). However, the cheaper, easier, and the most effective method by far is to fill the holes with the dog's own solid waste, then covering it with a thin layer of dirt. Dogs do not like to get that on their paws, so imagine your dog's unpleasant surprise of returning to a favorite hole only to claw into his own mess. Don't worry — you won't have to leave this out in the yard for long, only until he gets redirected to the good digging spot.

"I'm totally digging it!" — Creating a digging spot in your yard

Reserve a place where your dog can dig to his heart's content. It doesn't have to be very large, just wide and deep enough for him to make himself a cool spot for stretching out, or bury a favorite toy. It can be a patch of dirt or sand, but distinctly different from the type of ground cover you want him to avoid. Enthusiastically bring him to this area and encourage him to be near it. Praise him if you see him start to dig and let him see you dig in it with your hands or a tool. Let him see you bury some treats in shallow holes, and praise him for digging up those treats. Repeat sessions like this until he gets the idea, which shouldn't take long because you're training him to do something he wants to do! For more complete instructions, read the section on teaching "Find It" in Chapter 6.

Destruction/Chewing

No, the new cushions were NOT dog toys!

If your dog is chewing your yard into a shredded mess, you're not alone in your frustration! Dogs can do an enormous amount of damage to things you would have never considered a chew toy ("Really, Horace — ANOTHER sprinkler head?!"). In battling this problem, you should first figure out why your dog is chewing everything in sight. There are basically three reasons: Youth, habit, or boredom/anxiety.

Is this simply a normal puppy stage? Dogs are driven to chew from the time they are puppies to about two years old. It's a developmental stage that coincides with maturation and gaining their adult teeth. The worst of this chewing stage is from roughly 8 months to 1.5 years old, which is why a puppy who has never been a problem chewer before can seem to suddenly become one. It's really important to identify if your dog is in this stage so that you can understand it's not deviant, aggressive, or oppositional behavior — it's just your dog doing what his body is urging him to do. And if this is the case, perhaps the best thing you can do is to limit your dog's access to valuable items until he is through this phase. You might consider removing/ storing your wooden furniture, chair cushions, and other chewable yard components until your puppy has grown out of this stage. By providing a smaller area that is separate from the rest of the yard, with fencing or a kennel, you offer the flip side of the same solution. Either way, ensure your dog is getting plenty of exercise during this growth phase. By exhausting his puppy energy, you will reduce his drive to chew and dig. Make sure you also supply your dog with plenty of chew toys and dog bones so he can indulge his urges with your approval. As he approaches 1.5 to 2 years old you can start slowly increasing his access to the whole yard and yard furniture until he has worked up to a non-destructive attitude towards both!

When you catch your dog in the act of chewing something she shouldn't, it's good to have a "Leave it" command trained to put a stop to the chewing immediately. This command can be used in many situations in addition to chewing — to stop her from grabbing food off the table, trying to steal food or a toy out of a child's hand, bothering a cat or other animal, or going through the trash to name a few.

Is this an established habit in an adult dog? A dog will continue destructive chewing out of habit if you do not address the puppy chewing mentioned above. What starts as a physical urge while they are maturing can become a behavioral habit if it is left unchecked. The problem is corrected in exactly the same way as with puppy chewing, but it may take longer because the chewing is so ingrained in the dog's routine.

Is this an indication of boredom or anxiety? If you have an adult dog (2 years or older) who has not previously been destructive and you suddenly find him tearing up cushions or eating your wooden chairs, you probably have a bored or anxious pooch. Has his routine changed recently? Did you reduce his exercise or the amount of time you spend with him daily? Did something in your family change? Did he lose a play friend (another dog, a cat, or any other animal to which he used to have access)? These are all changes that can trigger obsessive, destructive behavior. Do your best sleuthing to figure out what, if anything, has caused his state of mind and what you can do to improve it. If he is simply bored, try to increase exercise and your interaction with him. If he is reacting to a loss of a person or another animal, think about how that loss affects him and find ways to fill that void.

Digging in the right spot

If you catch your dog in the act of digging, give a verbal correction and then excitedly bring him to the "approved" digging spot. Praise him when he steps foot on it.

Leave It

Put your dog on a leash, ideally attached to a correction collar. Put something on the ground that you know your dog will want to put in her mouth but that she shouldn't take, like a plate with human food or a child's toy. Allow her to approach it, and as she goes to take it give her a strong correction and say "Leave it!" If she stops and looks up at you, praise her and give her a dog treat for listening. If she ignores you, correct her again and repeat the command until she stops trying to get the item. Once you are successful in getting her to avoid the item and you have rewarded her, use the leash to take her back to the item again. Repeat this process again and again until she can be right next to the item without trying to take it. It is important do this exercise until she ignores the temptation instead of removing it from her reach. Set up sessions like this once a day for many days until you can take her to something tempting, say "Leave it," and she ignores the item without having to be corrected.

Bolting

Teach your dog to stay at home (even if the gate is left open)

"Bolting" refers to a dog running away from his property if and when he gains access to the front yard from either the home or the backyard. From a petscaping point of view, this can be prevented by creating a physical barrier like an actual fence around your front yard or an underground dog fence system. Both are very effective and the decision of which to use comes down to price and appearance, with the electronic fence being potentially more expensive to install and maintain.

Behaviorally, the best approach is to train a dog not to bolt either instead of or in addition to the physical barrier. This can be tackled with a combination of off-leash work and boundary training, both of which can be started with a dog as early as 8 weeks old. In fact, the earlier the better since a young puppy will naturally follow you around closely, whether inside or out.

Begin by teaching your dog a strong "recall" command, which means he comes running back to you when you say "Come" or call his name. This is important not only because the boundary training is built on the recall, but because you need a command to get him back to you if the boundary is broken! It's easy to do, but it does take a while for a dog to get a strong, reliable recall. Allow yourself 4 weeks of at least one session a day (allow more time if you only work it a few times a week). Some dogs learn it more quickly, some take significantly longer, but you should see some results in this period of time.

Training a Recall

Outdoor recall training involves a 20-foot line and some dog treats. You can purchase a long leash, or make your own training line by attaching a metal leash clip to a piece of cotton laundry line. I actually prefer the second option because it's lighter and therefore better for training this command. It's also a less expensive option; both the clip and the laundry line can be found at any hardware store for a few dollars total.

You'll want to use small, low fat treats because you'll be giving your dog many over the course of this training. I always suggest using the dog's regular kibble as the treat, and just deducting that amount from his meal later so he doesn't get overfed. Wear clothes with a pocket where you can keep the treats, or use a fanny pack or similar pouch so that you're not trying to train with a handful of treats. You want to be able to easily reach in and grab just one every time your dog earns it.

One is the loneliest number

If you catch your dog in the act of digging, give a verbal correction and then excitedly bring him to the "approved" digging spot. Praise him when he steps foot on it.

Trusted Treats

When using food rewards to train your dog, try using his regular kibble instead of other types of dog treats. Measure how much you use for training and deduct that from his daily serving so he doesn't get overfed. The kibble is healthier than higher fat, higher calorie doggy treats and won't turn your dog into a fussy eater the way treats can.

Outside, attach the rope to your dog's collar and remove the regular leash. Let the dog run about, giving him time to forget about the rope. You will be holding the end of the rope, but at the 25ft distance, and without ever letting him feel tension. Once he's settled down a bit, call his name and "Come!" If he comes, give lots of praise. If he doesn't, give a quick, sharp tug on the line and repeat "Come!" Once he's to you, praise like crazy and give a treat sporadically. While training this command, teach your dog the acceptable boundaries on your property when not within the confines of a fence. Decide exactly how far he is allowed to roam in your front yard by calling him back to you every time he is about to cross a boundary.

Once you've reached the point where he is coming to you as soon as you say "Come!" and you're not correcting anymore, start phasing out the rope. You will do this by first dropping the end of the rope and letting your dog drag it, while remaining close to the end of it should you need to reach down and grab it or step on it for a correction. As he becomes reliable, you'll start trimming off length from the rope, 5 feet at a time, but maintain your 20-foot distance. This gradual removal of the rope eliminates the chance your dog will suddenly notice he's off leash and bolt.

The Growling Gatekeeper

Battling inappropriate fence and yard aggression

Whether you have a 100 pound guard dog or an 8 pound Chihuahua, your dog is probably fiercely loyal to you and territorial about his wonderful home. It is natural for dogs to bark and growl at strangers entering their yard, a great feature for deterring unwanted intruders, but a problem for your gardener, gas meter reader, pool man, etc. The very best solution for avoiding problems is to confine your dog to your house or his kennel before a service person arrives. The friendliest dog might give a territorial bite, and the most responsible gardener can accidentally let your dog escape through an open gate; confining your dog protects you from both scenarios.

If you have an enthusiastic guard dog who threatens your service people, but confining him beforehand is not an option, evaluate your dog's temperament to determine if it is reasonable to address this situation strictly with training. You can work with your dog to be more accepting of specific intruders, such as the weekly pool man, without losing his guarding abilities. This is only appropriate if:

- Your dog has never bitten or snapped at anyone

- Your dog is normally non-aggressive

- Your dog is friendly towards new people outside his yard

- The service person is comfortable around dogs and willing to help with training

If your dog does not fit all of the above criteria you need to physically separate him from your service people.

Some dogs are fence-aggressive, meaning they try to attack people or animals on the other side of their fence. It may seem desirable to have your yard guarded in this way, but if your fence borders a sidewalk, alley, street, or pathway where there is likely foot traffic and your dog can fit his snout through your fence, we highly recommend discouraging this behavior. It poses a safety threat to your dog, the people or animals on the other side, and a liability threat to you if someone should get hurt by your dog as a result. In Chapter 1 we talk about different fencing options; one way to prevent fence fighting is to install a more solid fence. Alternatively, try blocking your dog's access to the fence with landscaping. Plant thick, hardy bushes or vines that spread laterally for good coverage. Planting foliage with thorns will further detract your dog from pushing up against the fence. Refer back to "Hedges" in Chapter 1 for specific recommendations when selecting your plants.

Go Say Hi

Train your dog to accept a service person by introducing the person to your dog in a very positive way. You should set this up to mimic the potential problem situation, so have your dog in your yard to start. Enter with your service person through the same door or gate that will normally be used. Be cheerful as you greet your dog and let him see you being cheerful and relaxed with your service person. Dogs take their cues from us, so if he sees you think this person is okay, he will think that too. Instruct the person to offer his hand out to your pooch while holding a treat. Say "Go say hi" and encourage your dog to take the treat. Praise him if he does it non-aggressively and give extra praise if your dog allows the person to pet him (if he exhibits any type of aggressive behavior, sternly reprimand him until he stops). Repeat this as many times as it takes for your dog to approach this person in a friendly manner. Once he does, give the service person more treats and have him enter again without you being with him. At this point your dog should associate this person with treats and praise, and greet him happily. Once trained, you can ensure optimal success by leaving a small container of treats outside your yard where your service person can get them each week. If he grabs a couple before entering the yard, he can reward your dog's friendly greetings with both praise and treats. Your dog will look forward to his visits in no time!

Controlling Pests Your Pet Detests

Fleas and Ticks:
A flea circus may be amusing to children, but it's no fun for your pet!

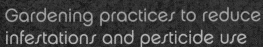

Fleas and ticks are the most common insects that may "bug" your dogs and cats. Fleas can cause medical issues in pets including flea allergy dermatitis (FAD), hair loss due to scratching, tapeworms, and secondary skin irritations. An infestation left untreated can cause anemia from blood loss, especially in puppies and kittens. Ticks can also transmit serious diseases, including Lyme Disease, Ehrlichiosis, and Rocky Mountain Spotted Fever.

Both types of parasites are often lurking outside in the brush, waiting for a tasty host (your dog or cat) to walk by so they can jump on for a blood meal and a warm place to sleep. One female will lay about 20 eggs per day, and up to 600 in her lifetime, so infestation can be a rapid process if left untreated. As they can be found in virtually every climate, taking preventative measures to keep them at bay is highly recommended, even if you have never seen a flea or tick on your pet. For excellent prevention and control in high flea population environments, couple the methods below with an insect growth regulator (or IGR) which prevents flea eggs and larvae from becoming jumping, biting adult fleas.

The following guidelines will help reduce flea and tick populations, as well as those of various other critters that might be freeloading in your garden (snakes, spiders, rodents, roaches, etc).

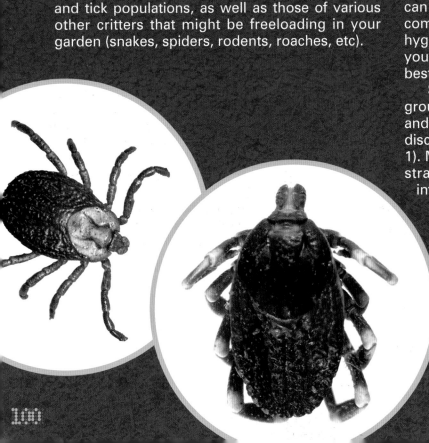

Gardening practices to reduce infestations and pesticide use

Good planning and garden maintenance practice can help control pests in your yard and reduce the need for insecticides (chemicals that kill bugs and can be dangerous to people and pets). Using a combination of landscape maintenance, good pet hygiene, health care, and repellents should keep your pest problems at a minimum and keep your best friend as happy as she can be.

Start with the yard perimeter. Inspect your grounds to ensure the fencing is in good shape and free from tears, gaps, or holes (for a detailed discussion of fencing, please refer back to Chapter 1). Maintaining a good sound fence will help keep stray animals from visiting your property and infesting your yard.

Lawns and ground covers should be kept mowed or clipped and not allowed to go to seed. A well manicured lawn inhibits wild animal visitors. Tall or messy vegetation offers hiding places for many animals and makes them feel secure about crossing your property (especially at night) or living in your backyard. Once tall grasses and weeds go to seed they provide a food source for flea-carrying rats, mice, squirrels and other grain feeding animals. Keep the flower beds neat and shrubs pruned of dead

▲ *A well manicured garden with infrequent watering naturally reduces pest infestations.*

material. Regularly collecting leaf debris reduces earwigs, pincher bugs, and pill bugs (roly-polies). It also reduces opportunities for bugs to hide and nest. Mulching the garden with pre-composted material helps with moisture retention, weed abatement, and can provide housing for predator beetles (desirable insects who feed on the pests you don't want).

Watering frequency will greatly affect insect populations in the garden. Watering less often, but deeper is good for plants, and also helps reduce garden pests like fleas, ticks, snails and mosquitoes. Biting insects like mosquitoes can irritate your pet and carry infectious viruses and they thrive in a wet environment. Monitor your garden and make sure there are no stagnant pools of water as these can be breeding grounds for mosquito larvae.

Planting the garden with shrubs that are known to work as natural insect repellents such as Peppermint, Lavender, and Lemon offer year long beauty and the added benefit that you can take the oils or juices from these plants and rub them into your dog's fur to help repel ticks and fleas. Lemon or rosemary oils can be dabbed on your pet's collar. Also known to be helpful are the oils from Cedar, Eucalyptus and Rosewood.

When life gives you lemons... Make flea repellent

You can safely and easily make your own flea repellent from ingredients found in your own backyard. Cut about 6 lemons in half or use several springs of rosemary (for those of us who don't have lemon trees in our back yards), and steep in a liter of boiling water for a few hours. Strain the liquid into a spray bottle and spritz your pet's fur and carpets.

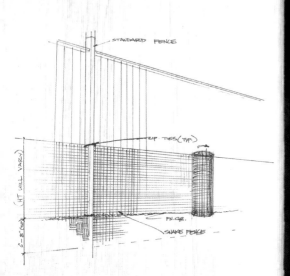

STANDARD FENCE

ZIP-TIES (TYP.)

(HT. WILL VARY)

6'-8" DEEP

FN. GR.

SNAKE FENCE

Snake Fence

Snake fencing is simply rolled galvanized metal mesh fencing material with smaller holes tied to your existing fence. Snakes find it difficult to climb this type of fencing, especially when 3-4 feet tall. To install it properly, dig a trench 6-8 inches deep and set the bottom of the fencing below grade. This will help prevent snakes from easily digging under your fence. Then using plastic zip-ties or tie-wire, attach the mesh fencing to your existing wrought iron or chain- link fence. Be sure to compact your trench to complete your installation.

Snakes in the garden: Don't let them rattle your nerves

Homes located in rural areas or bordering on nature preserves or parks, may be at risk for snake visitations. Most common snakes do not pose a risk to your dogs or cats as they are small and non-poisonous. They can even be helpful in ridding your yard of garden-destroying rodents. But if venomous snakes are indigenous to your area, you could reduce a pretty serious risk to your pets with just a few simple precautions.

Choosing a block wall for your yard will eliminate nearly all of a snake's access; the solid design prevents slithering through everywhere but under the gates. Yard entry is very simple through any other type of perimeter, so if snakes are a pest in your neighborhood, consider installing a "snake fence" around the perimeter of the property. This type of fencing is also helpful in controlling rabbits.

Snakes like to nest in warm, dark, dry, protective spots such as wood piles, junk piles, and overgrown foliage. Protect your pet from a surprise encounter by keeping your yard free of such debris. Follow the guidelines for yard maintenance at the beginning of this chapter to reduce overgrown areas of vegetation where snakes like to live.

Bee gone!
The buzz on bee and
yellow jacket abatement

Flying pests can be a nuisance to your dog, especially if they're the stinging kind like bees and yellow jackets. The insects are not attracted to your pets specifically; it's more that your pet may get stung or bit by wandering too near whatever is attracting the insects. In the case of bees, it's flowers. Refrain from placing your pet's food and water bowls near high-nectar flowers. If you start to notice an unusually high number of bees flying around your yard, inspect the property for hidden hives. If one is discovered, call an exterminator who specializes in bee and wasp abatement to have it safely removed.

Where yellow jackets are a problem, hang traps around the perimeter of the yard (they can be found at any hardware or home store). Yellow jackets are attracted to fruit or meat, depending on the point in their life cycle; if you are battling a Yellow Jacket population, avoid feeding your dog meats or moist dog food outdoors.

snake abatement training

Many people are afraid of snakes, but many pets are not. Most folks will stay clear of snakes when encountered in the garden, but dogs will often approach with curiosity and may attack unless trained to do otherwise. Rattlesnake aversion training, often referred to as "snake breaking" or "snake proofing," has been proven safe and very effective in helping to prevent dogs from being bitten by rattlesnakes. Check your local listings for companies that offer this quick and affordable service. One session per year with an experienced professional will offer your dog valuable protection.

Slaying the slime: Snail control

Common garden snails and slugs are a real pest across most of the country. Gardeners are at a constant war with these voracious, moving stomachs from the mollusk family. While quietly hiding most of the day, snails and slugs come out at night to devour your favorite plants and flowers, making the garden look unsightly.

To kill snails in the yard many gardeners turn to poisonous baits. Snail baits sold in stores are basically stomach poisons and they are extremely dangerous for dogs and cats! Baits look just like kibble when wet and can be mistaken as food by your pets. Some dogs will even eat dead snails that have been poisoned by baits and become ill themselves. Snail bait ingestion is one of the most common poisonings in dogs, and it takes very little (only one teaspoon for small dogs) to cause death.

The best organic method to control snails in the garden is to set traps with pie tins or plastic cups filled with a little stale beer. Beer? Yes, snails are attracted to beer and the slimy creatures fall into the traps and get caught easily. Expect to catch 4-6 snails per night per trap. If your dog gets to the beer first, consider burying plastic cups down into the ground. Hate the idea of wasting beer on snails? Visit your garden during the night donning a pair of gloves with a flashlight and collect the snails from your plants for disposal later.

Snails thrive on decaying plant material. To reduce snail and slug populations in your garden, keep leaf debris raked up and remove old leaves from plantings. They also like a moist environment so you can hinder their success by watering less often, allowing soil to dry in-between irrigation sessions.

▼ *Snails have a reputation for moving slowly, but did you know they can cover the distance of a football field overnight? To make matters worse, snails can multiply rapidly as they are asexual and require no mate to reproduce.*

▲ Coyotes are formidable in the field where they enjoy keen vision and a strong sense of smell. They can run up to 40 miles (64 kilometers) per hour.

▲ ScareCrow® sprinkler head
by Contech Electronics

Be wary of Wylie:
Coyote threats to pets

These adaptable animals will eat almost anything. They hunt rabbits, rodents, fish, frogs, and even deer. Because they also kill family pets, many home-owners regard them as destructive pests.

Coyote populations and pet attacks are on the rise. They are becoming emboldened to tread into suburban backyards. Coyotes have no problem jumping fences or digging under them. Although attacks on people are rare, coyotes are often attracted to dog food and animals that are small enough to appear as prey. Unsecured pet food and uncollected garbage can attract these predators into your yard.

If your home is adjacent to coyote habitat, you'll need to take extra precautions to protect your pets. Steps to consider:

1. Provide a dog run with a complete enclosure atop to protect from predators.

2. Install "Coyote Roller Fencing" at the top of your perimeter fence. These roller bars foil coyote attempts to get a foothold and limit access to your yard

3. Install clever "Scarecrow" motion activated sprinkler heads to chase unwanted visitors out of your yard. Each unit costs under $100 and protects a 40 foot wide area.

4. Secure pet food stations outdoors.

5. Use trash receptacles that are tamper proof.

6. Supervise your smaller pet when outside, especially at night

Creative Ideas
for Pets Who Don't Bark

Photo by Deidra Walpole

DOGS

may be the most common type of outdoor pet, but they are surely not the only animals sharing our yards. This chapter caters to those of us who have house cats, birds, reptiles, exotics, and even welcomed wildlife enjoying the digs within our fence lines. The information covered throughout this book applies to a variety of pets, and can guide you through yard and garden design no matter what kind of animals you have.

Here kitty kitty kitty!
Garden considerations and cat houses

Whether your cat lives strictly outdoors, or spends only a portion of her day outdoors, she will appreciate some special kitty accommodations. Cats thrive when they have access to the outdoors, and this doesn't need to mean prowling the neighborhood. There are many risks to a cat with unlimited roaming, including moving vehicles, aggressive animals, hazardous locations, unfriendly humans, parasites and diseases. You can successfully design your yard so kitty can run, play, explore, lounge, and sun herself outside while preventing her from leaving the safety of home.

Fencing. Cats are great climbers and gifted contortionists. To keep one from getting past a fence it need be tall (at least 6 feet, ideally 8 feet or taller) and difficult to climb. For example, a smooth, solid block wall is much harder to escape than chain link. It must make contact with the ground to prevent squiggling under, with gaps no wider than 2" to prevent sneaking through. Wrought iron fences should be altered to have smaller gaps and the alteration should extend the full height of the fence. Cats do especially well with underground dog fence systems, buried electrical fences that use a mild electric shock to correct a cat from going past your yard's boundary. Consult Chapter 1 for more information on both these types of fences.

Meeting kitty's needs. All the basics regarding shelter and water discussed in Chapter 3 apply to your cat as well. Cats are fastidiously neat, and will expect you to provide very fresh water. For this reason, cats really appreciate the aerated water of a fountain as their water source. There are outdoor shelters designed specifically for cats or simply choose a small to medium sized dog house. Shelter location is very important, as cats can be private or shy animals that want to be tucked away from the crowd. They also like to survey their surroundings from a safe spot, so ideally you would mount your cat's kitty house 3-5 feet off the ground. This is especially important if they are sharing the yard with dogs.

Just as your cat likes her litter box inside, she will prefer having a designated sandy potty spot outside over trying to find a place to go. This can be an actual sandbox or simply a pile of sand in a secluded corner of the yard. Be sure to clean this area often, as you would an indoor litter box. This is obviously not recommended for families with small children who might play in the sand.

Photos courtesy Mike Kaufman

Garden treats: Cats eat plants and vegetation to provide themselves with vitamins and minerals and to help with digestion. They will ingest grass and chew on many of the plants in a garden. If you do not want your cat snacking on specific plants, we recommend planting a patch of garden just for the kitty. Cats are skilled at avoiding poisonous varieties, but to be safe, consult the list of toxic plants (Appendix B) before making your choices.

Edible feline favorites

Keep your garden safe and your kitty happy by planting her a garden of her own. Be sure to include some type of grass and catnip. Other favorites include Catmint, Thyme, Sage, Parsley, Rosemary, Alyssium, and Heather.

Creative touches such as this concrete paver tortoise and crossing gate add whimsy and fun to your PETSCAPED garden.

For the slowpokes:
Tortoise/Turtles enclosures

Turtles and tortoises are much more likely to remain happy and healthy if kept outside. The delicate balance of heat, sunshine, and water they require is very difficult to reproduce indoors, but create a safe outdoor enclosure and Mother Nature takes care of all that! It is important to determine first if your species can acclimate to your geographical climate. If so, you can have fun designing anything from a basic enclosure to a deluxe turtle paradise.

A good turtle or tortoise enclosure consists of sufficient protection to keep your pet in and keep predators out. There are many animals that pose a threat, including birds of prey, raccoons, possums, coyotes, and good old dogs and cats. The area need not be fully enclosed, though this provides the maximum level of protection. Additional features to include are a den box, a shaded area, a basking area, and a water source he can dip into. The more aquatic varieties will need a pond or pool big enough for swimming, with a basking rock in the middle and a gentle slope for entering and exiting. We recommend enclosures be at least 15 feet from side to side, and bigger if you have multiple or very large animals.

They may look sweet and innocent, but these guys can eat an entire garden in no time (the tortoise, not the host!). Design a special tortoise area with edible plants for him that is separate from the lush landscaping of your yard. (Brandon Johnson from HGTV's "Get Out, Way Out" with the Kirschnew family tortoise)

Be warned: Turtles and tortoises love greenery! They will enjoy the lettuce and carrots you put out for them, but they'll devour your decorative plants as well. Choose plants that are hardy, grow quickly, and of course, are non-toxic. With a little attention to detail, you can create a beautiful and delicious garden for your pets to enjoy in multiple ways.

Decorative pets:
The beauty of Koi ponds

Waterfalls and ponds offer many benefits to home garden design and continue to grow in popularity. These graceful water features add visual interest as focal points in the backyard. The sound of a properly installed waterfall creates a relaxing ambiance that is sure to reduce your stress. Placed appropriately, the white noise from a waterfall can be used to screen noise pollution from highways and offensive neighbors.

For the Petscaped garden, waterfalls and ponds are a decorative way to add another water source in the yard for dogs and cats as well as to provide a home for one of our favorite pets, Koi fish. Koi provide colorful visual interest for all other garden guests. They are amusing to watch swim and interact with each other. Koi are available in a variety of bright colors and decorative patterns. Both adults and children enjoy watching the colorful fish and Koi can be easily trained to eat right out of your hand.

Train your Koi to handfeed:

Koi can be easily trained to swim up and take food directly from your hand. To teach this behavior, approach the pond slowly at feeding times so you don't frighten or startle the fish. In the beginning, they may hide under stones and moss, but after a time they will begin to link your presence with feeding time. Keep the fish hungry by avoiding over-feeding during training periods. Allow your hand to move over the water and then lightly sprinkle feeding pellets into the pond a few at a time. The idea is to get the fish comfortable with the presence of your hand. Each day, move your hand closer to the water. Soon, as you approach the pond, the fish will begin to swarm to you at feeding time and clamber to eat right out of your hand! Handfeeding fish is an exciting activity for both kids and adults.

▲ *Koi fish are the symbol of Love and Friendship in Japanese culture.*

Ponds attract flying visitors

Another benefit to having a waterfall and pond in your own backyard is that they welcome a variety of flying visitors to the garden. Expect to see birds of all colors and sizes bathing in the pond as well as visiting dragonflies and hummingbirds. Unfortunately, not all birds are welcome visitors. Larger birds, like herons, can be an unwelcome predator as they will actually eat smaller Koi and goldfish. If these larger birds become a pest in your garden, consider placing a "Scarecrow" motion activated sprinkler head adjacent to the pond. Many of our clients have successfully used these automatic battery operated sprinkler heads as guardians of their ponds.

▼ Koi hobbyists claim that the inclusion of one all black Koi fish amongst the other colorful fish in a pond is good luck. The black color is reminiscent of the black ink used by ancient Japanese scribes.

You can tune a waterfall, but you can't tuna fish!

The sound created by moving water can be relaxing and sooth the nerves. It can also be reminiscent of noises heard in the toilet and encourage the need to pee. Some water features are so loud they agitate you rather than relax you. As you build your waterfall, be aware of the different sound effects created as water passes over different stones at varying heights. For instance, water cascading over a flat flagstone in a sheet will create much more noise than water gurgling around and over cobblestones. Taller falls create more of a crashing sound. Single thin streams of water can sound like urination in a toilet. You can move stones around in your waterfalls to create different pleasing sound effects and actually "tune" your waterfall and pond.

Go wild!
Attracting wild birds and butterflies

Birdbaths and bird feeders will turn any yard into a wildlife preserve! What better way to surround yourself with beautiful color and enchanting song than by inviting a variety of birds over for food, drink, and a bath? Your dog will be equally entertained by the parade of feathered visitors in his yard, especially when he's out there by himself. Some dogs will simply watch, while others like to charge at them and attempt to grab the birds. No worries if your dog is this second variety; it is a rare dog that can catch a live bird, and the birds who frequent your yard will learn to anticipate the attack and fly just out of reach in plenty of time. Cats, however, are a whole different story! Attracting wild birds to yards with active, hunting cats is not recommended; they are skilled predators who enjoy catching prey for sport, even if they're well-fed.

Placement of a feeder or bath is key to enjoyment, so consider a few criteria when choosing your location. Regular wild birdseed will grow just about anywhere, and the seeds get flicked onto the ground surrounding the feeder when the birds feed, so the feeder should be placed with this in mind. Erecting a feeder in the middle of a well-groomed lawn will lead to a big patch of birdseed plants, which can overtake the grass. One clever, albeit pricey, solution to this is to purchase non-viable seed. Specialty feed stores and online sources sell birdseed that will not germinate if planted.

There is a vast variety of bird feeders available, as well as birdseed mixes to target specific types of wild birds. A little research into indigenous species of your area can guide you in choosing what type of seed to buy. Some feeders are constructed to deter squirrels; without one you can expect squirrels to eat the birdseed as much as the birds.

One specialty feeder that will be successful in any area of the country is a "finch sock." These can be found in pet and hardware stores and are to be filled with black thistle seed. Tiny, colorful songbirds called finches will take perches on these vertical mesh "socks."

Another specialty feeder of note is a hummingbird feeder. These sugar solution dispensers are designed to hang from trees or other structures so that hummingbirds can feed on the solution while hovering in midair. If you have both seed feeders and hummingbird feeders, place them at least 10ft apart from each other so the hummingbirds are not intimidated by the bigger birds.

Photos courtesy Diana Harris

Butterflies: Plantings that attract butterflies to entertain cats and dogs

Butterfly gardening has become a popular hobby among "Petscapers." Fluttering through the garden, colorful butterflies provide a dazzling air show and entertain both you and your pets.

Keeping your dogs and cats occupied can help keep them from looking for other trouble. If you have a bored pet that is constantly getting into mischief, consider adding a butterfly garden to help keep your pet entertained during the day.

To attract more butterflies in your garden, simply plant shrubs and flowers that these insects find appealing. Plant your butterfly garden in a sunny location that is sheltered from wind. Butterflies won't feed where they have difficulty hanging on. Select plantings that are known to grow wild in meadows in your area.

Window views

Choose brightly colored flowering shrubs that are full of nectar to attract butterflies, songbirds, and hummingbirds; they will fly just outside your home's view windows. Favorites include; Butterfly Bush (Buddleja davidii), Purple Coneflower (Echinacea purpurea), and Bleeding Heart (Dicentra spectabilis, or Dicentra eximia). Train flowering vines around the frames of your windows, like honeysuckle vines (Lonicera sempervirens), or Confederate or Star Jasmine (Trachelospermum jasminoides). Don't forget to cross reference the poisonous plant list at the end of this book before selecting plantings.

It is important to note that attracting butterflies means providing a food source when they are in a caterpillar stage as well. Gardeners need to be tolerant of chewed leaves and stems on plants during the caterpillar life cycle. The use of insecticides will counter any efforts you have made to bring butterflies into the garden. Sometimes people forget that we need the caterpillar in order to have the butterfly. The great comedian George Carlin said it best, "The caterpillar does all the work, but the butterfly gets all the publicity!"

In addition to having plenty of high-nectar flowering plants you need to provide an easy access water source for butterflies. Place several shallow bird baths or a fountain in the garden to entice butterflies and song birds to visit your garden regularly.

Pet Safety Checklist

Detecting disasters. If you've ever wanted to be a detective, here's your chance! Whether you are moving into a new house and yard or you have been in your spot for a while, examine your yard the *PETSCAPING* way to look for potential problems and hazards you can fix before your animals get out or get hurt.

Safety
what danger lurks...

- **Injury Hazards.** Walk the perimeter of your grounds from a pet's perspective. Evaluate your fence, furniture, and tools and toys that are kept out for injury potential. Look closely for things like shredded or pointed wood, jutting wire or metal sheeting, nails and screws sticking out from surfaces, and heavy items propped up in such a way that they could get knocked over by wind or an animal.

- **Chewing temptations.** If your dog tends to chew excessively, check for signs that he is chewing your fence; chain link will grind down teeth and wood can be chewed through completely to make an exit.

- **Houdini's secrets.** Look for potential escape routes such as holes beneath a fence to crawl under, missing slats in a fence to squeeze through, and piles of things to climb up and then jump over your fence.

- **Fences**. Check if you have a potential for fence fighting between your dog and one on the other side. If there is a dog next door or your yard borders a sidewalk, would your dog be able to put his muzzle through the fence to fight with another dog? If so, take steps to prevent this possibility by altering the fence or planting a border of hedges (Chapter 1).

- **Poisonous Plants**. Use the list in this book to confirm you do not have any toxic plants or plant material in your yard. If you have a garden and you grow any of the toxic food items on the list, make sure your garden is completely dog-proof so your dog can't get at the canine poisons.

- **Pesticides**. If you are a do-it-yourselfer, be careful not to use pesticides where your animals can ingest them. Many pesticides, such as rat poison, are flavored and scented to entice ingestion; these will attract your pets and are lethal to them as well.

- **Exterminators**. If you use an extermination service, make sure water and food bowls are out of the spray's way, and that they know not to place poisons where your animals have access.

- **Dangers of snail control**. Be careful how you or your gardener control snails; snail bait ingestion is one of the most common poisonings in dogs, and it takes very little (only one teaspoon for small dogs) to cause death.

- **Pool and pond safety**. Make sure any ponds have a shallow ramp or steps so animals can escape if they jump or fall in. Make your pool animal safe with an exit ramp (Skamper Ramp) or a protective fence designed for pets as well as children (Guardian pet fencing).

Poisonous Plantings

10 Most Common Poisonous Plants & Other Toxic Plants

Courtesy of www.earthclinic.com/Pets/poisonous_plants.html

Marijuana. Animals who attempt to snack on this plant can suffer serious consequences such as diarrhea, vomiting, increased heart rate, drooling, in-coordination, and even possibly seizures and coma.

Sago Palm. While the seeds and nuts of this plant are most poisonous, the entire plant is toxic. Animals ingesting parts of this plant may suffer from diarrhea, vomiting, depression, seizures and liver failure.

Lilies. Plants of the lily variety are very poisonous to cats. Even very small amounts of this plant could cause serious kidney damage.

Tulips. The toxic portion of this plant is the actual bulb, which can cause drooling, central nervous system depression, gastrointestinal irritation, cardiac issues and convulsions.

Azalea. The toxins in azalea plants can be very severe and potentially cause drooling, diarrhea, vomiting, central nervous system weakening and depression, and in some cases possibly coma or death.

Oleander. All portions of this plant are poisonous and can cause gastrointestinal irritation, hypothermia, heart problems and possibly death.

Castor Bean. Poisoning as a result of this plant can cause abdominal pain, drooling, diarrhea, vomiting increased thirst, loss of appetite and weakness. More serious cases could also lead to dehydration, tremors, seizures, twitching muscles, coma and possibly death.

Cyclamen. The most poisonous portion of this plant is located in the root. Ingestion of the plant can cause severe vomiting and gastrointestinal irritation. In some cases death has been reported as a result.

Kalanchoe. Ingestion of this plant can cause gastrointestinal irritation and cardiac rhythm and rate problems.

Yew. Poisoning as a result of the yew plant can affect the nervous system and cause in-coordination, trembling and breathing difficulties. It may also result in gastrointestinal irritation, cardiac failure and could possibly lead to death.

The following is a list containing many other well-known and common plants that can be poisonous or toxic to pets.

Aconite. A garden flower whose roots, foliage and seeds can be poisonous.

Apple. The seeds of an apple can be poisonous to pets.

Arrowgrasses. Marsh type plants whose leaves contain poisons.

Atropa Belladonna. A type of garden herb in which the entire plant can be poisonous to pets, especially its seeds and roots.

Autumn Crocus. A commonly found garden flower in which the entire plant can be poisonous.

Baneberry. A wildflower whose berries and roots are the poisonous portions.

Bird of Paradise. A garden flower whose pods are poisonous.

Black Locust. A tree in which the entire plant can be poisonous, especially the bark and shoots.

Bloodroot. A wildflower and herb whose stem and roots are most poisonous, however the entire plant is toxic.

Box. An ornamental shrub that is poisonous in its entirety, but especially the leaves.

Buckeye. A tree whose sprouts, nuts and seeds contain poisons.

Buttercup. A wildflower and garden herb that is poisonous in its entirety but mostly in the leaves.

Caladium. A houseplant that is poisonous in its entirety.

Carolina Jessamine. An ornamental plant whose flowers and leaves contain poisons.

Chinaberry Tree. A tree whose berries are poisonous.

Chockcherries. A wild shrub whose poisonous parts include the leaves, cherries and pit.

Christmas Rose. A garden flower that contains toxic leaves and rootstock.

Common Privet. An ornamental shrub whose leaves and berries can be poisonous.

Corn Cockle. A wildflower and weed whose seeds are particularly poisonous.

Cowbane. A wildflower and herb that is poisonous in its entirety, especially the roots.

Cow Cockle. A wildflower and weed whose seeds are poisonous.

Cowslip. A wildflower and herb whose entire plant is poisonous, especially the leaves and stem.

Daffodil. A garden flower whose bulbs are poisonous.

Daphne. An ornamental shrub that contains poisonous bark, berries and leaves.

Death Camas. A field herb whose poisonous parts include the leaves, stems, seeds and flowers.

Delphinium. A wildflower that is poisonous in its entirety, especially the sprouts.

Dumbcane. A houseplant and is poisonous in its entirety.

Dutchman's Breeches. A wild and garden flower whose roots and foliage are poisonous.

Elderberry. A tree whose poisonous parts include the leaves, bark, roots and buds.

Elephant's Ear. A houseplant poisonous in its entirety.

English Ivy. An ornamental vine that is completely poisonous but especially the leaves and berries.

European Bittersweet. A vine poisonous in its entirety but especially in the berries.

False Flax. A wild herb whose seeds are poisonous.

False Hellebore. An ornamental flower whose roots, leaves and seeds are toxic.

Fan Weed. A wildflower and herb whose seeds are poisonous.

Field Peppergrass. A wildflower and herb that contains poisonous seeds.

Flax. A wildflower and herb whose seedpods contain poisons.

Foxglove. A wild and garden flower whose leaves are poisonous.

Holly. A shrub containing poisonous berries.

Horsechestnut. A tree containing poisonous nuts and sprouts.

Horse Nettle. A wildflower and herb poisonous in its entirety, especially the berries.

Hyacinth. A wild and houseplant whose bulbs are poisonous.

Iris. A wild and garden flower whose leaves and roots are poisonous.

Jack-in-the-Pulpit. A wildflower that is entirely poisonous, especially the leaves and roots.

Jatropha. A tree and shrub whose seeds are poisonous.

Jerusalem Cherry. An ornamental plant whose unripened fruit and foliage are poisonous.

Jimsonweed. A field plant that is entirely poisonous, especially the seeds.

Laburum. An ornamental plant whose seeds, pods and flowers can be poisonous.

Lantana. A houseplant whose foliage is poisonous.

Larkspur. A wildflower that is poisonous only as a young plant.

Laurels. A type of shrub with poisonous leaves.

Lupines. A shrub whose seeds and pods are poisonous.

Manchineel Tree. A tree containing poisonous sap and fruit.

Matrimony Vine. An ornamental vine containing poisonous leaves and shoots.

Mayapple. A wildflower poisonous in the form of its un-ripened fruit as well as the foliage and roots.

Milk Vetch. A wildflower poisonous in its entirety.

Mistletoe. A houseplant with poisonous berries.

Monkshood. A wildflower poisonous in its entirety, especially the roots and seeds.

Moodseed. A vine whose fruit and roots are poisonous.

Morning Glory. A wildflower containing poisonous seeds and roots.

Mountain Mahogany. A shrub with poisonous leaves.

Mustards. These are wildflowers whose seeds can be poisonous.

Narcissus. A garden flower whose bulbs contain poisons.

Nicotiana. A garden flower whose leaves are poisonous.

Nightshade. A wildflower and vine with poisonous leaves and berries.

Oaks. Are trees with poisonous leaves and shoots.

Philodendrons. Are houseplants poisonous in their entirety.

Pokeweed. A field plant containing poisonous roots, seeds and berries.

Poinsettia. A houseplant with poisonous leaves, flowers and stems.

Poison Hemlock. A field plant containing poisonous leaves, stems and fruit.

Potato. A garden plant whose shoots and sprouts can be poisonous.

Rattle Box. A wildflower that is entirely poisonous.

Rhododendron. An ornamental shrub whose leaves are poisonous.

Rhubarb. A garden plant with poisonous leaves.

Rosary Pea. A houseplant whose seeds are poisonous.

Skunk Cabbage. A marsh plant whose entire plant is poisonous but especially the roots and leaves.

Smart Weeds. Wildflowers containing poisonous sap.

Snow-on-the-Mountain. A wildflower whose sap is poisonous.

Sorghum. A type of grass whose leaves are poisonous.

Star of Bethlehem. A wildflower poisonous in its entirety.

Velvet Grass. A variety of grass whose leaves are poisonous.

Wild Black Cherry. A tree with poisonous leaves and pits.

Wild Radish. A wildflower with poisonous seeds.

Wisteria. An ornamental plant containing poisonous seeds and pods.

Woody Aster. A wildflower whose entire plant is poisonous.

Yellow Jessamine. An ornamental vine that is entirely poisonous.

Yellow Pine Flax. A wildflower poisonous in its entirety but especially in the seedpods.

Surprising Household Hazards to Dogs and Other Pets

Chocolate can stimulate the nervous system and is poisonous to all species of dogs.

Grapes and raisins can cause damage to the kidneys.

Garlic and onions can damage the red blood cells and cause anemia in dogs.

Xylitol found in sugarless gum causes lower blood sugar and can cause vomiting and seizures in dogs.

Raw yeast and bread dough can cause gas in the digestive track and result in alcohol poisoning. Poisonous to all species but only dogs will typically ingest enough of it to cause harm.

Macadamia nuts can cause muscle and nervous system problems in dogs.

APPENDIX B Poisonous Plantings

Edible Gardens for Pets

Anthea Davidson,
*Creative Horticultural Consultant
& Garden Designer
www.EdibleGardenDesigns.com*

When I arrive at client's house I am nearly always greeted by

a friendly pet. The dog is overjoyed and looking for attention and the cat smooches my legs giving me "approval." I won't even talk about the fur and slobber left on my black trousers after a day of consulting!

But it made me think. These animals are like a family member—they like a varied, healthy diet to keep them in the best possible shape. Their well-being is important to their owner and the pet needs an animal-friendly garden.

So let's think about practical garden designs that can be shared and enjoyed by owner and pet together. Most importantly, how to incorporate plants that pets can eat or rub against to gain the essential vitamins and minerals needed for a shiny coat, good digestion and fewer allergies, making a happy, healthier pet!

Cats

In my experience, people spend far more on plants for their cat than for their dog.

Catmint, cat thyme and **cat grass** are the most common herbs used for cat health and wellbeing.

Catmint: This bears a spectacular lavender-like flower spike and green to greyish foliage. It's good as a low groundcover for hot dry spots. It's extremely drought tolerant, too. Catmint looks great mass-planted under roses—it creates a carpet effect.

Cats love it because it has a hallucinogenic effect! Cats rub against it or nibble at it releasing a chemical called Nepetalactone. You will see the cat bouncing around, rolling on the ground, and possible drooling. It's a little like the behavior you see in a human after a few glasses of wine!

Catmint is also excellent for repelling mosquitoes and even cockroaches. So plant it near your outdoor entertaining area.

Cat grass: This is a cereal grass which eliminates furballs by making the cat vomit. It is also high in vitamins and minerals. This is best kept in pots as it looks a little "weedy."

Cat thyme: The aromatic foliage on this 1 meter high plant is eye-catching. It is very silver and likes a hot spot. It can be kept pruned to create a low hedge effect. It has dainty pink flowers. Cats love the aroma and you'll see them smooching this plant.

This is a good herb to pick and dry. Place it into a breathable bag and put it on your cat's bed. It is calm and soothing and will give your cat sweet dreams!

These cat herbs are all fantastic in pots, too. Leave them near the back door where cats are likely to hang around.

If yours is an indoor cat, the plants can also be kept indoors in a bright sunny room for short periods. Just remember to use organic sprays only on plants your animals may eat.

Dogs

Unfortunately there are more toxic plants out there for dogs than edible ones. Dogs do enjoy eating **ferns**, especially those beautiful juicy sweet new shoots, and gnawing on **bamboo**, both mainly safely edible.

The number one favorite for dogs is lavender—but watch out for the bees!

Lavender has a lemony taste to it. Lots of varieties are available for garden uses, including Spanish, Italian, French, and English.

English lavender is commonly used for its striking grey foliage and is great in hedges and for potpourri. The others have showy flowers with aromatic foliage and look good planted in clusters of 3 or 5 (yes, keep them in uneven numbers for best effect!). They also do well in pots. As I mentioned, bees love them so they are great for bringing bees into your edible garden for pollination.

Lavender is a great aromatherapy product for dogs, as it is humans. It is commonly used in dog treats, for shampoo and to keep fleas at bay—and that's just for starters.

Positive Pet Corners

Serious animal lovers can devote a corner or small section of their garden to their pet. Plant all the edible, perfumed plants your animal loves. It can be used for rewarding positive behavior when dog training, for one thing. Your dog would be allowed to enter this area after a successful training session to tantalize the senses and relax it—and it could also be an alternative to a food treat.

Edibles as a Deterrent

Edible plants can also be used to deter animals from garden beds or even steer them away from unsafe areas.

Although we love our pets, sometimes there are certain areas which we like to see remain animal-free.

I often hear clients complaining about their dogs creating a muddy track through the garden or trampling through a manicured box hedge, leaving a gaping hole every time this happens.

Many clients give up on planting an area because "it's the dog's digging area" or "it's where the cat goes to the bathroom."

Well there is a solution.

You can change animal behavior by planting these areas with plants that release an aroma or oil that is distasteful to the pet. Some of these are edible and some are ornamental, but both give either flower or foliage interest to the landscape.

Here are some examples I've found popular: edibles such as marigolds, nasturtiums, chives and basil are not liked by cats and dogs due to their aroma and sharp tasting foliage.

Coleus cannis, commonly known as "dog's bane," is an impressive looking succulent plant that is not only hardy but bears a lovely lavender-like flower spike in the cooler months. Dogs hate it—and won't go near it!

The added bonus with a lot of these edibles is they also help to keep away insects that may cause skin, eye, and ear irritations in our pets.

Pest Control—and a Safety Barrier, Too!

Here's another bonus. Consider using herbs that may help prevent unwanted pests. For instance, the perfumed citronella geranium releases an oil that is an attractive mosquito deterrent. It's perfect for those damp areas or around the kennel or cat run!

The culinary herb fennel helps prevent fleas on cats and dogs. It also makes a very trendy kitchen salad! I make one with green apples, chicken, green onion and fennel, tossed with a horseradish dressing.

The herb feverfew and artemisia help to control insects. Feverfew has soft lacy limey leaves. Artemisia, part of the daisy family, is soft, fluffy, and grey in color. They have great foliage effects when planted as a mass.

Every edible flower a dog eats—such as pineapple sage, hibiscus, carnations, or pansies—is high in vitamins. They can also be used in the cooking of doggy treats.

Thorny edible plants may also be used as a deterrent for unsafe areas such as steep banks, screening off pool equipment, or to prevent dogs jumping onto fences. We can use edible canes such as raspberries or blackberries, with caution.

About EdibleGardenDesigns.com

www.EdibleGardenDesigns.com was created for the growing band of people who want to harvest their own food to stay healthy and save money but who want well-designed gardens, too—not just a traditional vegetable patch!

ABOUT Anthea Davidson

Anthea is a creative horticultural consultant and designer. She has more than 20 years' experience in the retail horticulture and design industry with a multi-award winning garden nursery. After the birth of her two sons, she established her own garden consultation and design business to give her more time flexibility. (Her sons have enjoyed helping in the garden since they could walk.) Anthea's clients appreciate her creative flair, her down-to-earth knowledge on a vast array of plants and their care, and her ability to get inside her clients' heads to help them create the perfect garden for their home.